PSYCHIATRIC PREVENTION AND THE FAMILY LIFE CYCLE
Risk Reduction by Frontline Practitioners

72539

Report No. 127

PSYCHIATRIC PREVENTION AND THE FAMILY LIFE CYCLE

Risk Reduction by Frontline Practitioners

Formulated by the
Committee on Preventive Psychiatry

Group for the Advancement of Psychiatry

BRUNNER/MAZEL *Publishers* • New York

Library of Congress Cataloging-in-Publication Data

Psychiatric prevention and the family life cycle : risk
    reduction by frontline practitioners / formulated by the
    Committee on Preventive Psychiatry, Group for the
    Advancement of Psychiatry.
        p.   cm. — (Report ; no. 127)
    Bibliography: p.
    ISBN 0-87630-548-6
    1. Mental illness—Prevention.   2. Developmental
psychology.   3. Family psychotherapy.   I. Group for the
Advancement of Psychiatry. Committee on Preventive
Psychiatry : 1984) ; no. 127.
    [DNLM: 1. Family.   2. Family Therapy.   3. Mental
Disorders—prevention & control.   W1 RE209BR no. 127 /
WM 100 P97453]
RC321.G7 no. 127
[RA790.5]
616.89 s—dc20
[306.874]
DNLM/DLC
for Library of Congress   89-7252
                                                                      CIP

Published by
BRUNNER/MAZEL, INC.
19 Union Square West
New York, New York 10003

MANUFACTURED IN THE UNITED STATES OF AMERICA

10   9   8   7   6   5   4   3   2   1

STATEMENT OF PURPOSE

THE GROUP FOR THE ADVANCEMENT OF PSYCHIATRY has a membership of approximately 300 psychiatrists, most of whom are organized in the form of a number of working committees. These committees direct their efforts toward the study of various aspects of psychiatry and the application of this knowledge to the fields of mental health and human relations.

Collaboration with specialists in other disciplines has been and is one of GAP's working principles. Since the formation of GAP in 1946, its members have worked closely with such other specialists as anthropologists, biologists, economists, statisticians, educators, lawyers, nurses, psychologists, sociologists, social workers, and experts in mass communication, philosophy, and semantics. GAP envisages a continuing program of work according to the following aims:

1. To collect and appraise significant data in the fields of psychiatry, mental health, and human relations;
2. To reevaluate old concepts and to develop and test new ones;
3. To apply the knowledge thus obtained for the promotion of mental health and good human relations.

GAP is an independent group, and its reports represent the composite findings and opinions of its members only, guided by its many consultants.

Psychiatric Prevention and the Family Life Cycle was formulated by the Committee on Preventive Psychiatry. The members of this committee are listed on page vii. The members of the other GAP committees, as well as additional membership categories and current and past officers of GAP, are listed at the end of the report.

The editorial assistance of Harriette D. Borsuch
and James D. Gwyn is gratefully acknowledged.

CONTENTS

PSYCHIATRIC PREVENTION AND THE FAMILY LIFE CYCLE
Risk Reduction by Frontline Practitioners

1

INTRODUCTION

This document will address psychiatric prevention by focusing on the earliest manifestations of developmental deviations throughout the personal and family life cycles. Our goals are therefore twofold: 1) to promote or maintain the mental health and well-being of individuals within the family unit; and 2) to prevent the onset of psychiatric disorders or dysfunctions which would threaten the stability and well-being of the family unit.

The means of accomplishing these goals are to identify potential risks at each family life cycle stage and then to provide specific risk reduction techniques that are developmentally appropriate for each stage. These preventive interventions are designed to be implemented in a diversity of settings and by a range of frontline practitioners. Such settings include: schools, churches, the home, primary care settings, daycare centers, community meeting places, athletic and recreational programs for youth, welfare offices, and so forth. Frontline practitioners include: teachers, coaches, nurses, clergy, police, physicians, lawyers, social workers, psychologists, daycare workers.

Some 30 million people in the United States—about 15% of the population according to the Multi-Center Epidemiological Catchment Area Study of the National Institute of Mental Health (NIMH) —suffer from diagnosable mental illness (Klerman, 1986). We are thus dealing with a public health epidemic. Although mentally ill persons usually do not die from their illness, most of the over 30,000 suicides a year are related to some mental disorder.

Most mental illnesses usually are not caused by extraneous agents or solely by some inborn factor but are to a considerable extent the end-manifestation of human development gone awry. This is currently an unpopular view of mental illness. But mental disorder does not arise in a vacuum; it is the outcome of pre- and postnatal developmental vicissitudes which, if corrected or ameliorated as early as possible, might not have resulted in the gross maladjustments diagnosed as mental illness.

Can mental disorders be prevented much as smallpox has been prevented? If that were possible, not only would the distress that mental illness now causes to so many Americans and their families be eliminated, but the United States would save billions of dollars a year from reduced medical costs and would gain by the individual's improved productivity. Unfortunately, prevention of mental illness is more complicated than that of infectious disease. There is no inoculation against mental illness and there probably never will be. There usually is no single and necessary cause against which to concentrate preventive efforts, either by blocking a particular agent or through raising specific defenses. While some symptoms may have a modified biological mechanism, the majority of syndromes are more likely the product of complex interactions between constitutional and experiential variables.

In this sense, mental disorders are more like cancer and heart disease, both of which may result from a combination of factors including behavior and habitual patterns such as diet or smoking. Constitutional predispositions and lifestyle factors are very important in the development of mental illness, and both are difficult to modify; so the prevention of all mental illness is probably an unrealistic goal. However, to prevent even a modest fraction of such disorders or reduce morbidity would be a tremendous boon to the entire nation.

Retrospective studies (Grob, 1985) provide some evidence that at least a portion of mental illness can be prevented. The psychosocial aspects contributing to mental disorders can usually be traced back to attitudes and occurrences in an individual's early life, although the presence of these attitudes and occurrences does not always lead—prospectively—to later mental disorder. Studies such as those by Chess and Thomas (1984) have shown that a substantial portion of people predisposed to developing mental dysfunction through early family and environmental attitudes and vicissitudes have been able to overcome their impact and achieve mental health. The keys to preventing mental and behavioral disorders lie in identifying and reducing risk conditions early in the child's life and in the ongoing relationships with adults.

Disordered human relationships can create risk conditions for children, endangering healthy growth and development. Adults responsive to children's individual needs provide opportunities for the establishment of coping skills by creating an atmosphere conducive to emotional growth and learning. The intimacy shared in a family is a key element in these growth-facilitating aspects which will impact on subsequent activities and later relationships in the neighborhood, schools, religious institutions and other social settings.

It is often overlooked, or taken for granted, that basic capacities—learning how to relate to others, feeling secure, acquiring self-esteem, enjoying closeness and intimacy with others, feeling motivated to learn and to grow, distinguishing fantasy and imagination from shared ideas or percepts, and postponing gratification without undue stress—depend predominantly on experiences in human relationships. The configurations of human relationships vary, but they always begin with a primary relationship, usually with the mother and her immediate surroundings. This early human development in a family of whatever composition is therefore where clinical attention and knowledge can discern risk conditions and recommend prevention measures, even if there is no complaint or diagnosis. But in order to promote mental health and reduce risks for mental disorders and to help families modify attitudes and avoid possible injurious behaviors, access to families must be gained before maladjustment begins.

Although in the course of treating individuals and families, psychiatrists and other mental health professionals have many opportunities to make preventive interventions, they are usually at least one step removed from settings where risk conditions can be identified and preventive measures most effectively instituted. Opportunities for such activities occur in primary care settings, particularly in pediatricians' or family physicians' offices, during home visits by public health nurses, in the clergyman's study, in the social services office, in daycare centers and schools. This report, therefore, is directed not only to mental health professionals, but even more to *those who provide primary care and those who are in other ways strategically placed to help children get a fair share in life: the frontline caretakers and practitioners.*

Preventive medicine and the safeguarding of health have concerned modern nations for over a century. Such concepts were promulgated concisely by no less a scientist/physician that Rudolf Virchow, the father of cellular pathology and a European social activist in the mid-1800s. He asserted that medicine ultimately is a social concern and discipline involving the political apparatus. The verity of this statement has been demonstrated again and again. Through the work of Edward Jenner, vaccination against smallpox became feasible two centuries ago, but the worldwide eradication of this dread disease had to wait until our time because of resistance due to inadequate education and superstitious beliefs, and because of a dearth of resources. Similarly, Jenner's battles for acceptance of his vaccine have been repeated again and again in other spheres: the battle for fluoridation of water to prevent dental caries is still not won completely.

Currently we see resistance to eliminating tobacco from our lives stemming from economic and political considerations; ideological opposition to programs of family life and sex education; and pennywise and pound-foolish policies undermining programs such as Head Start. The last two projects subserve the conservation of human potential, which requires that children be wanted, valued and well-nurtured physically and emotionally in order to grow to their full potential—in David Hamburg's (1985) words, to reduce the casualties of early life.

Prevention in the field of mental health has been conceptually oversimplified by some scientists and practitioners and oversold by others. Hopes for a simple preventive were reinforced when pellagra was successfully eliminated and subsequently prevented through better diets. Likewise, hopes were reinforced by the prevention of neurosyphilis through penicillin. However, the notion that there ought to be a vaccine or serum against this or that psychiatric condition is based on the erroneous belief and hope that all diseases conform to the tuberculosis model, a disease that cannot occur without the invasion of the tubercule bacillus.

Specificity between toxin and antitoxin had been the basis for the original model of primary prevention in public health practice. However, illnesses conforming to this infectious disease model of prevention are no longer the most significant health problems. They have been replaced by chronic diseases such as diabetes or arthritis which currently cannot be prevented but can be treated rather effectively. Dennis J. Tolsma (1983) of the Centers for Disease Control has stated, "In the prevention model, health can more and more be seen as a normal state we can maintain, by actions that it is within our own capability to take . . . by decisions we can make, or require our democratic institutions to make. We call this idea 'health promotion and disease prevention.' " We, therefore, eschew the term or concept of "primary prevention" in its original sense and focus on risk reduction at the earliest opportunity as a more appropriate preventive concept in the mental health field. Such an approach includes health promotion.

A goal of this report is to supply frontline practitioners with basic observational guideposts and intervention techniques to address some of the more commonly seen deviations from the broad range of healthful family functioning. Our hope is that the interventions we describe may serve as examples and/or stimulation for frontline personnel to attempt commonsense risk-reducing interventions to guide the family toward optimal individual and family development. Such interventions are designed to occur early in the sequence of events that ultimately lead to full expression of individual and family dysfunction.

We recognize the tremendous sociocultural variations and economic diversity in the United States and elsewhere. Social disorganization, poverty and serious illness are significant risk conditions for the family. This report, however, focuses mainly on families with relatively adequate income, housing and education because the basic vicissitudes of human development can be more clearly highlighted in families without gross social or economic disadvantages. Moreover, it is not our intent to present new findings or recent research per se, but to demonstrate how current knowledge based on past research and clinical experience can be applied in preventive and remedial action and programs.

HELPING THE CHILD GET AN OPTIMAL START

Inheritance and Fertility Management

Reducing the risk for mental illness requires, first of all, increasing the proportion of children who are healthy and wanted. Young people who are sexually active need to ask themselves if they are willing and ready to take on the responsibility to bring up a child. Good nutrition, good housing, and a family with adequate financial and personal resources are important positive factors for raising healthy children. Explicit parental decision and agreement to reproduce, judicious spacing of children through appropriate family planning, and informed acceptance of parental roles are basic to propitious family life. Availability and utilization of prenatal services are crucial to the health care of the mother and newborn for reducing risks of low birth weight, prematurity and other maldevelopments. Some obvious and tangible risks for a fetus are intrauterine infections such as venereal disease or AIDS and drug or alcohol abuse by mothers-to-be. Important preventive measures for newborns include testing for phenylketonuria and other inborn errors and metabolism.

Genetic counseling, ideally before conception, is crucial, especially when the parents are concerned that there is some risk for a genetic anomaly. The issue of inheritance of mental illness has been controversial for many years. In the late nineteenth and early twentieth centuries the eugenics movement used questionable data to recommend sterilization for the mentally retarded and the mentally ill. Considering the appalling use to which the Nazis put the pseudoscientific conclusions of the eugenicists, that movement became discredited. Also discredited because of their methodological weaknesses were early inheritance studies. With the increased enthusiasm for psychodynamics, the role of heredity in mental illness was virtually ignored for several decades. Currently a more balanced view prevails in which the importance of multiple familial precursors in schizophrenia and affective disorders is recognized. In contrast to Huntington's disease, where a child is at 50% risk if a parent has the disease, inherited predisposition to most major mental illnesses requires the impact of adverse psychosocial environmental factors to convert potential into manifest pathology. Biological predisposition of vulnerability may determine the nature of some symptoms, but the timing and perhaps the severity of a mental illness as well as its response to treatment are affected by psychosocial factors. Experiential factors appear to play a larger part, and biological factors a proportionately smaller part, in the more prevalent but usually less severe neurotic and personality disorders.

Parental Attitudes and Individual Differences

The family is usually the earliest and most important setting for psychosocial interaction and learning. Even such tangible preventive factors as proper nutrition of the avoidance of drugs, alcohol and tobacco during pregnancy are to a considerable degree the outcome of attitudes learned in the family. The more intangible elements—love, trust, tolerance and internal controls—are usually developed within the context of the family and are related to parental attitudes and relationships. Preventive psychiatry therefore seeks to promote harmonious family functioning and helpful parental attitudes and behaviors, and also to modify potentially damaging practices.

Methods of attempting to modify parental attitudes include the mass-marketing of books such as Benjamin Spock's (1961) *Pocket Book of Infant and Child Care* or T. Berry Brazelton's (1985) *On Becoming a Family*, the distribution of pamphlets in doctors' offices, newspaper articles, and television shows. These are relatively inexpensive ways of providing information, but are not as effective in modifying attitudes as one would hope. Such approaches are likely to have the most impact on those who need them the least.

Television is an important vehicle for information and education for children, adults and the family. However, it is also a risk source. Programs depicting violence, cruelty and sexual promiscuity aside, television can be misused as an impersonal babysitter as well as an inadequate substitute for reading or active play or sports by both adults and children; indeed, its overuse can preempt family interaction.

Another problem with mass-marketing methods is that they tend to encourage stereotyping. Parents look for specific guidelines, and no matter how carefully an author tries to point out the range of responses and behaviors that can be expected from a child at a given age, many people will read into the material that there is a single most desirable achievement and a single most desirable type of behavior for each stage of development. Consequently, problems may be perceived where no problems exist. The pernicious myth of perfection can thus begin its sinister path early in a child's life.

Stereotyping can be a problem for professionals, too. In the past mental health professionals have not paid adequate attention to individual and cultural diversity, or to the differences in temperament which seem to be a part of a child's biologic makeup. Chess and Thomas (1984) and other investigators have provided data that take these differences into account and emphasize individuation in the management of child-parent problems. Furthermore, formulations are often made as if families regularly consisted of the basic triad of two parents and one child. Insufficient attention has been directed to the family as a system, to the significance of siblings in a family, to single-parent families, to families affected by death, divorce or poverty, or to families in which both parents are employed. We must be aware of and respect the importance of different lifestyles, family composition, and cultural values and traditions; wherever possible in this report, these variations will be noted and discussed. However, the principal family functions and tasks and individual developmental milestones, early ones in particular, are basically the same the world over regardless of family composition or cultural, religious or ethnic differences.

Clinics and Primary Care

Child guidance clinics and similar agencies have attempted to modify parental attitudes as well as to treat troubled children. In the 1920s and 1930s, the pioneers in child guidance hoped that intervening early in the course of an emotional disturbance would prevent later, more serious problems. The results of these attempts to prevent mental illnesses have been disappointing, possibly because the focus was primarily on the child. Parents were seen separately and concepts of clinical work with the family as a group did not exist. Also, children and their families tended to be referred after a problem had become established rather than earlier in its course, so that the best opportunities for prevention or risk reduction had passed. However, these clinics did establish the principle of interprofessional teamwork, now considered rather routine in therapeutic and preventive endeavors.

Primary care professionals do see "patients" for checkups who may have neither complaints nor a diagnosis. The most widespread of these encounters are at well-baby clinics, school health surveys (often limited to eye and ear examinations), office visits for immunization, and health checks as a requirement for employment. Premarital examinations or tests could be used to check the couple's general health—mental health included—and, through brief interviews, also discuss sexual issues and plans for parenthood. Health maintenance organizations (HMOs) could provide preventive services, but for the most part they do not do so for financial reasons, which often restrict their mental health services as well. These professionals are on the frontline, so to speak, and they can and need to assess risk conditions. As change-agents they can prevent continued stagnation or maldevelopments in individuals and in families.

IMPEDIMENTS AND BARRIERS TO PREVENTION

For over a century public health experts have asserted that a part of health resources should be allotted to the prevention of illness.

Since World War I emotional and psychological disorders and dysfunctions have been included in this outlook. However, an adequate mandate and financial support for prevention and health promotion have never been achieved. For instance, although it has been demonstrated that the incidence of high-risk pregnancies and birth problems can be reduced, that sociocultural mental retardation is largely preventable, and that children's age-appropriate competence in relating to others can, to some extent, be enhanced, many pregnant women and children fail to receive necessary care. Despite a host of publications, commissions, and task forces devoted to prevention, actual implementation of programs is lacking and training for mental health personnel in these areas is still very sketchy (Buckner et al., 1985).

Therefore, we shall highlight some possible reasons for the delay in developing preventive programs and offer some suggestions and approaches that may promote their implementation. Two broad categories of impediments and barriers to the implementation of prevention are 1) operational and 2) sociocultural. As will become readily evident, the components within these broad categories are not mutually exclusive. Operational impediments include definitional issues, lack of knowledge, the quest for evidence of effectiveness (cost-effectiveness in particular), ethical considerations, and deficiencies in school and other social systems beyond the ambience of the mental health or medical professions. Sociocultural resistance exists in individual, familial, communal, professional and political spheres.

Operational Impediments

As noted, the complexity of the currently known causative or contributory factors involved in mental illness renders specific protection and prevention difficult if not impossible. The methods or interventions to avert mental disorders, dysfunctions or handicaps are based on clinical experience and on epidemiological surveys. Clear proof of preventive effectiveness, or risk reduction, requires multigenerational prospective studies, which are forbiddingly expensive in terms of time and professional resources. Another impediment to the effective implementation of preventive services relates to how those services are defined, which in turn governs reimbursability through conventional health insurance or governmental payment systems.

Experts recognize the combined influence of psychosocial, biological and hereditary influences that place people at increased risk for the development of psychiatric and mental disorders. Despite this, only a few research projects or pilot programs to screen for, and possibly protect, high-risk populations have been instituted (Albee, 1979; Robins, 1978; Rutter, 1979). Of course, the assignment to high-risk status does not, in and of itself, mean that such an individual will develop a clinically diagnosable disorder. Special attention to or continued clinical surveillance of such cohorts would likely help reduce individual risk status. Most experts recognize the significant interplay of socioeconomic factors that may serve either to protect an at-risk individual from developing a clinical disorder or to exacerbate the risk(s).

Most proposed interventions cannot address a specific disorder in the traditional sense of primary prevention; the aim thus is to minimize or alleviate abnormal reactions to stressful life events and/or to improve coping skills in an attempt to prevent disorders or dysfunctions associated with difficult living conditions.

Prevention in the mental health area thus needs a new paradigm, for often what we are attempting to prevent are not specific disorders, but the long-term psychophysiologic and psychopathologic effects of continued or recurrent stresses and imbalances in the internal and external environments. Different people react to stressful life events with very different responses: some with physical illness, others with emotional illness, and still others with no apparent ill effects or with even enhanced coping skills. Outcome depends in part on individuals' genetic and constitutional predisposition, their temperament, their attribution of the events (blaming themselves or extraneous factors), whether they perceived themselves as able to cope, and on familial and communal supports. The age of the individuals and their developmental stage also affect how they interpret stresses and, as a consequence, how they will react to them. Factors in the environment such as the presence of a support network and someone to confide in are also important and may help to buffer the stress. George Albee (1979) has attempted to formulate these interactions and the outcome as follows:

$$\frac{\text{Organic Factors} + \text{Stress}}{\text{Competence} + \text{Coping Skills} + \text{Social Supports}} = \text{Outcome}$$

This formula reflects noxious factors above the line, and helpful and risk-reducing ones below. Their balance determines the outcome, namely, the prevention, or the eventual emergence, of mental and emotional disorder.

Questions as to whether prevention works and how we can prove that it works are difficult to answer. Funding agencies require evidence of cost-benefit and cost-effectiveness of preventive interventions, but the demonstration of effectiveness requires great skill, methodological rigor and finesse. These acknowledged difficulties more often have led to inaction than to either taking chances that a program will be effective or providing the funds for appropriate demonstration and control to discover effectiveness or its lack. In Bowlby's (1953) words, "To wait for certainty is to wait for eternity."

Ethical considerations about the potential invasion of privacy, or the tampering with self-choice, also impede preventive measures, particularly among minority or disadvantaged groups. Whether a prevention expert should be telling others what is best for them regarding family life and rearing practices, and in so doing possibly interfere with self-determination and cultural tenets and values, is an issue that must be addressed. Disease prevention and its corollary, health promotion, involve decisions affecting an individual's sense of self, lifestyle, freedom and future. How and when the message of prevention is delivered to an individual or group may well determine the degree to which it will be heard and responded to.

Another issue concerns the focus of responsibility for implementing prevention programs. Should health promotion and disease prevention be the responsibility of federal, state or local governments, health care professionals, religious organizations, employers, third-party payers, or community services? How should these concepts be reinforced throughout the individual's lifespan and in the settings of systems where people live and work? Further concerns relate to the value structure implicit in preventive activities and to society's right or responsibility to insist on health as important to its citizens—a value judgment not necessarily shared by all.

Lastly, labeling individuals as being at risk for a disorder before they express any complaints or symptoms may be not only unwelcome, but also potentially harmful by interfering in personal or familial efforts to cope with or rectify a risk condition, or accept it without undue anxiety. This concern is magnified when applied to mental disorders, which carry a social stigma in many people's minds. It is one thing to be told that you are at risk for diabetes and quite another to be told that you may become suicidal or psychotic. Such ethical and value concerns have been addressed and discussed only recently as they relate to the emergence of prevention activities in the mental health field (Bloom, 1982; Lamb & Zusman, 1981).

Sociocultural Impediments

At the individual level, we must consider personal resistances to practicing good prevention. These may include the natural tendency of any individual to feel invulnerable and not susceptible. People do not label themselves as being a member of a high-risk population even if a close relative is mentally ill. Individuals, young ones in particular, tend not to recognize risk-taking behaviors in which they engage nor to identify particular high-risk settings for the development of disorders and dysfunctions. Thus, they may not see problems as being potentially pathogenic.

Individual barriers also include lack of adequate education and basic health knowledge regarding the effects of trauma, physical illness, stressful life events, and the roles of exercise and good nutrition in healthy biopsychosocial functioning. Hence, if individuals are not presented with alternatives for more healthful lifestyles, they cannot be motivated to change. Individuals must be convinced that prevention requires only an "ounce" of personal investment, and not the "pound" that is often attributed to its alternative—treatment or "cure."

Preventive activities are mainly voluntary; hence, people may engage in some health-promoting activities but not in others. Individuals may perceive prevention as a series of many distinct activities or constraints that are unpleasant, not specific, and unproven. All of us tend to avoid making immediate sacrifices for the sake of attaining remote future goals, the more so if the goal is "negative" such as preventing something unknown from happening. There is little political or social groundswell demanding preventive services for mental illness, and it is hard to motivate people to accept help or advice before they themselves recognize a problem.

On the family level, the challenges to introducing preventive concepts and health promotion are numerous. Today in the United States a large number of families are blended or headed by single parents (more often women) or are in transition secondary to divorce, separation or death. The nuclear triangular family structure, although always a psychologic reality, no longer applies in fact to a large number of families. For this and related factors, families need to be considered at risk for the development of a range of emotional and psychosocial dysfunctions. Reconstituted or blended families are also at risk for the development of such disorders due to special and even confusing stresses, such as bridging several evolutionary family task stages simultaneously (see Chapter 2).

Children in our culture are regarded as primarily the responsibility of their parents, and no special knowledge or skill is considered requisite for becoming or being a parent. All too often children are not viewed as a resource for the future, and there is no concerted societal effort to safeguard the development of children. Hence, insufficient time, resources and attention are devoted to preventive efforts. In 1984, according to the U.S. Bureau of Census, one-sixth of our citizens lived below the poverty level, malnourished and often hungry (*World Almanac*, 1986). The children among them are especially at risk for all kinds of ill health, including stunted personal development. The barrier to risk-reduction is high sociopolitically, and so advocacy by our professions to remedy such adverse health factors must become a high priority.

Adequate and effective preparation for parenthood is essential to establishing wholesome families, and such preparation is especially critical for those young people who have not grown up in well-functioning families and/or communities. However, major resistances and many prejudices to extrafamilial teaching about, and support for, families may be encountered. This resistance shows most noisily and stridently around issues of sex education and pregnancy prevention. Although the preventive effectiveness of early family life and sex education in reducing undesired pregnancy, especially in teenage populations, has been demonstrated (Zelnick & Kim, 1982), there are many groups in this country who oppose programs, particularly in schools, that educate about sex. These groups claim that such teaching promotes and stimulates sexual activity among the young, or that it is the family's prerogative to teach about sex. But if families did or could accomplish this task effectively, we would not experience an epidemic of teenage pregnancies and abortions.

Prevention-resistive groups and organizations unfortunately often prevail with school boards and educational systems; they also often intimidate caretakers such as teachers, youth workers and even physicians. Surgeon General C. Everett Koop was criticized severely for advocating the advertisement and easy distribution of condoms for young people as a preventive against AIDS and other sexually transmitted diseases. If the family is the major humanizing agent of infants and children, and if this task depends on an appropriate level of competence, preventive efforts and programs must address the issue of how life begins, prevent the birth of children to children who cannot function as parents beyond feeding the infant, and overcome resistances to teaching about reproductive hygiene and parenthood responsibilities outside the family.

Because emotional and behavioral dysfunctions are so complex and multifaceted in origin, effective preventive programs must take into account the total ecological system in which children live. By being too narrowly focused and oversimplistic, many past attempts at prevention have failed because they attacked too small a facet of children's lives for too short a period of time to have any lasting effect against environments that were overwhelmingly stressful and constantly evolving. However, there are now enough convincing studies (Albee, 1978; Stone et al., 1981) showing that preventive interventions are not only worthwhile, but also cost effective. Tables 1 and 2 list representative examples.

Professionals also have accorded prevention a lower status than that attributed to the therapeutic and treatment arena. Professionals receive gratification from "curing" disease and relieving pain and suffering. These interventions are easy to measure over time and are clear and clean. By and large, health care practitioners are not educated with regard to the role they can play in providing preventive health services. Many primary care providers have not been taught the basic concepts of preventive health care and are often ignorant about the interplay between physical health and mental well-being. There is little if any instruction concerning family dynamics and functioning in most medical schools or in programs for other health professionals, with the possible exception of schools for training in social work.

Third-party reimbursement and other forms of health insurance do not reward the practitioners for preventive services or even

TABLE 1

Some Examples of Effective Risk Reduction Programs

Program or Intervention	Target Population
Premarital and marital counseling	Couples preparing for marriage, newlyweds or couples with marital problems
Genetic counseling	Prospective or established parents concerned about inherited or familial diseases
Prenatal care and birth preparation	Pregnant women and couples, if extant

Residential group care for unwed mothers and infants	Teenage and older single mothers in need of schooling or work preparation
Well-baby clinics	Infants
Home visiting by nurse	Infants, their mothers, or parents in need of support and help with infant care, e.g., of infants disturbed or defective or abused; families in unsafe housing, e.g., lead exposure
Foster care (supervised) and/or adoption	Unwanted, neglected, abused and institutionalized children
Daycare, nurseries	Children of working mothers or in need of supplementary care and stimulation
Warm lines	Parents in need of help and guidance
Hot lines	People in distress, e.g., unwanted pregnancy, addiction, suicidal preoccupation
Head Start	Preschoolers and parents in poor neighborhoods, slums
After-school programs	Children of working mothers (and fathers, if any)—"latch key kids"
Special school programs	Learning-disabled, retarded or truant children
School clinics	School population
Family life and sex education	All children appropriate for age, emphasis on pubertal and adolescent cohorts
Social skill and "refusal" training ("Just say no")	Elementary and secondary schools
Work-place health programs, especially as to substance abuse	Employees with performance decline and/or undue absenteeism
Single groups (Parents without Partners)	Isolates, divorcees, widows, widowers
Various "Anonymous" groups	Addicts motivated to forestall recidivism, abusive families
Crisis programs—outreach	Families beset by natural or man-made disasters, sudden deaths

TABLE 2
Cost-Effective Programs*

WIC: Food for Women, Infants, Children
  Reduces infant mortality and increases birthweight.
  Only 44% of those eligible participate.
  $1 investment in prenatal component can save $3 in short-term hospital costs.

Prenatal Care
  Reduces low birthweight, prematurity and infant mortality.
  $1 investment can save $3.38 in cost of care for low-birthweight infants.

Medicaid
  Decreases neonatal and infant mortality, and abnormalities through early
    periodic screening services.
  $1 spent on comprehensive prenatal care for Medicaid recipients saves $2 in
    infant's first-year care.

Childhood Immunization
  Reduces vaccine-preventable childhood diseases like rubella, mumps, measles
    and polio.
  $1 spent on childhood immunization program saves $10 in later medical
    costs.

Preschool Education
  Increases school success, employability and self-esteem. Less than 20% of
    those eligible are participating in Head Start.
  $1 spent on preschool education can save $6 in later social costs.

*House Select Committee on Children, Youth and Families, *New York Times,* Sept. 25, 1988

for spending time with individuals or families to identify and assess risk status. Thus, one of the biggest barriers to prevention remains the method of funding, which rewards the physician who provides brief assessment or treatment services, but pays less or nothing for educational counseling or for time-consuming consultations with other professionals such as teachers or preschool educators working with children and their families. Time is an important issue— mental health professionals in the private sector are reimbursed on a time-related basis, but other practitioners are not. Health workers, especially in the public sector, are often under severe time constraints. Advocacy by our professions for mandating payments for preventive services, including time spent on consultation and interagency contacts, is very much in order.

Other barriers to prevention include the role of community and social organizations that influence all individuals throughout their lifespan. There are different levels of responsibility and different levels of interaction between social organizations and individuals in our society. If we assume that good preventive intervention approaches cannot occur in isolation and must represent a confluence or integrative approach across social networks and settings, it is imperative that there be communication between and among these various social services.

Another barrier in the social sphere relates to the provision of the "necessary ingredients" or "basic requirements" in which preventive actions can be undertaken. Adequate housing, good education, access to health care, availability of employment, and insurance of safe environments in which to live, work and play are all basic needs as emphasized by the 1978 report of the President's Commission on Mental Health:

> The task Panel on Families singles out three issues for priority consideration in the work of the President's Commission on Mental Health:
>
> 1) Strengthen the role of the family in prevention, in the enhancement of mental health, and in the care of incapacitated members by, first of all, assuring basic structural supports of the family, including jobs, adequate housing, health care, education, recreation, security, and, in the absence of adequate job-produced resources, a guaranteed minimum income.
>
> 2) Provide, on a universal basis, a wide array of family support services required to prevent crises and to enable families to cope with crises when they occur. To the extent possible, services should be provided through families and the usual mediating agencies such as neighborhoods, schools, churches, voluntary organizations, and communities, with minimal reliance on specialized, extrafamily institutions.
>
> 3) Develop a new capability for study of mental health policies through the establishment of six university-based and independent policy research institutes, each specializing in a designated aspect of mental health, including studies of public policies affecting families and children; and develop a system for assessing the status of children in families through

improving governmental and nongovernmental data gathering
systems, and by refining and formalizing a system of social
indicators reflecting the status of children and families, and
their change over time. (p. 551)

SUMMARY

As has been noted by many in the field, it is often very difficult to
translate the philosophical belief that it is better to prevent a
problem than to cure one into terms that can be understood,
implemented and evaluated. If we start with the premise that it is
worthwhile, in and of itself, to improve the quality of life in the
general population, and especially regarding children, it is possible to begin the process of implementation. If the number of
adverse factors in the environment could be even minimally reduced
or children's competence increased, a significant decrease in the
incidence of some of the common childhood mental health problems could result. It is possible to intervene at any point in the life
cycle, but the relative merits of intervention at any one particular
point can be argued realistically, or rejected on the basis of traditions and beliefs. The relative merits of various interventions in
terms of the greatest good to the largest percentage of the population are therefore hotly debated. Focus can be on the individual at
different stages of development or on the family in its different life
cycle stages, on the family at times of crisis, on the subcultural
environment in which the family is situated, on the institutions and
agencies that impact the developing individual, and on the sociopolitical level. Intervention at any one of these levels may alter that
environment and subsequently facilitate more competent functioning by all the individuals involved.

Although family physicians and pediatricians are the guardians
of health and are well-equipped to identify risk conditions, other
professionals in the community also have such opportunities.
These primary care professionals have important strategic advantages over mental health specialists and agencies in reducing risks
for mental illness and in functioning as agents for change by

intervening early in nascent psychiatric problems. They have a natural entree, and their contacts with children and families give them ongoing opportunities to observe, evaluate and encourage patterns of interaction within the family that are likely to reduce the risks for mental disorders. Since they meet people in life cycle transitions and crises when the opportunities for preventive intervention are greatest, they can discourage pathogenic patterns either before they result in symptoms or before symptoms have become firmly established. Another important advantage that frontline personnel have is that usually families trust them and likely will accept recommended interventions. Furthermore, families can share problems with such personnel without loss of status or fear of the stigma which unfortunately is still widely associated in our society with seeking help from mental health professionals or agencies. However, the often uncritical acceptance by families of such interventions can put a burden on frontline practitioners, who need to be reasonably sure that their interventions are constructive.

This volume will present a systems view of basic family dynamics and structure and trace this unique human institution through its evolutionary life cycle. In subsequent chapters it will describe the typical tasks and functions as they pertain to individual and familial life cycle stages and identify normative attitudes and task pursuits as well as unwholesome risk factors which, unless attended to, could result in individual and family disorder or dysfunction. Such remedial attention and intervention based on identifiable risk factors in the family context are the keys to risk reduction for mental disorder, and for promoting wholesome development and relationships.

REFERENCES

Adams, G.R., & Schaneveldt, S.D. (1984). Primary prevention and the family. Part I. *Journal of Primary Prevention, 5,* 71–74.
Adsett, C.A., & Rudnick, K.V. (1978). Psychiatric liaison with family practice teams. *Psychiatric Opinion, 15,* 29–33.

Albee, G.W. (1979). Primary prevention. *Canada's Mental Health, 27*(2), 5–9.

Alten, L., & Britt, M.W. (1983). Social class, mental health and mental illness: The impacts of resource and feedback. In R.D. Felner, L.A. Jason, J.N. Motsugu & S.S. Farber (Eds.), *Preventive psychology: Theory, research and practice* (pp. 149–161). New York: Pergamon.

Anthony, E.J. (1980). Do emotional problems of the child always have their origin in the family? In P. Brady & K. Brodie (Eds.), *Psychiatry at the crossroad* (pp. 97–115). Philadelphia: W.B. Saunders.

Ashford, N.A. (1987). New scientific evidence and public health imperatives. *New England Journal of Medicine, 316*, 1084–1085.

Bahnson, C.B. (1983). Individual and family response to external and internal stress. Proceedings of the Seventh World Congress of Psychiatry, Vienna.

Bleuler, M. (1974). The offspring of schizophrenics. *Schizophrenia Bulletin, 8*, 93–107.

Bloom, B.L. (1982). Advances and obstacles in prevention of mental disorders. In H.C. Shulberg & M. Killilea (Eds.), *The modern practice of community mental health* (pp. 126–147). San Francisco: Jossey-Bass.

Borus, J.F., & Anastasi, M.A. (1979). Mental health prevention groups in primary care settings. *International Journal of Mental Health, 8*, 58–73.

Bowlby, J. (1953). *Child care and the growth of love.* Harmondsworth, England: Penguin Books.

Brazelton, T.B. (1981). *On becoming a family. The growth of attachment.* New York: Delacort/Seymour Lawrence.

Broskowski, A., & Baker, F. (1974). Professional, organizational, and social barriers to primary prevention. *American Journal of Orthopsychiatry, 44*, 707–719.

Buckner, J.C., Trickett, E.J., & Corse, S.J. (1985). *Primary prevention in mental health: An annotated bibliography.* Department of Health and Human Services Publication (ADM) 85-1405.

Chess, A., & Thomas, A. (1984). *Origins and evolution of behaviors disorders: From infancy to early adult life.* New York: Brunner/Mazel.

Children's Defense Fund. (1982). *America's children and their families.* Washington, DC: Author.

Coleman, J.V., & Patrick, D.L. (1976). Integrating mental health services into primary medical care. *Medical Care, 14*, 654–661.

Eisenberg, L. (1981). A research framework for evaluating the promotion of mental health and prevention of mental illness. *Public Mental Health, 96*, 3–19.

Eisenberg, L. (1984). Rudolph Virchow, where are you now that we need you? *American Journal of Medicine, 77*, 524–532.

Engel, G. (1977). The need for a new medical model: A challenge for biomedicine. *Science, 196*, 129–136.

Fleck, S. (1975). Unified health services and family-focused primary care. *International Journal of Psychiatric Medicine, 6*, 501–515.

Grob, G.N. (1985). The origins of American psychiatric epidemiology. (Public health then and now). *American Journal of Public Health, 75*, 229–236.

Group for the Advancement of Psychiatry. (1980). *Mental health and primary care.* New York: Mental Health Materials Center.

Hamburg, D.A. (1985). Reducing the casualties of early life. A preventive orientation. *The president's essay. Annual report.* New York: The Carnegie Foundation.

Harmon, D.K., Holmes, T.H., & Masunda, M. (1969). The social readjustment rating scale: A cross-cultural study of Western Europeans and Americans. Presented at the Annual Meeting of the American Psychiatric Association, Bal Harbour, FL.

Hennon, C.B., & Peterson, B.H. (1981). An evaluation of a family life education delivery system for young families. *Family Relations, 30,* 387-394.

Hetznecker, W., & Forman, M.A. (1977). Developmental issues and minor psychosocial problems. In D.W. Smith (Ed.), *Introduction to clinical pediatrics* (2nd ed.). Philadelphia: W.B. Saunders.

Klerman, G. (1986). The NIHM epidemiologic catchment area progrm (ECA). Background, preliminary findings and implications. *Social Psychiatry 21,* 159-166.

Lamb, H.R., & Zusman, J. (1981). A new look at primary prevention. *Hospital and Community Psychiatry, 32,* 843-848.

Lebensohn, Z.M. (1975). Pilgrim's progress, or the tortuous road to mental health. *Comprehensive Psychiatry, 16*(5), 415-426.

Lewis, J.A., & Lewis, M.D. (1981). Educating counselors for primary prevention. *Counselor Education and Supervision, 20,* 172-181.

Lumsden, D.P. (Ed.) (1984). *Community mental health action: Primary prevention programming in Canada.* Ottawa: The Canadian Public Health Association.

McGinnis, J.M. (1985). The limits of prevention. *Public Health Reports, 100,* 255-260.

Mengel, M.B. (1987). Physician ineffectiveness due to family-of-origin issues. *Family Systems Medicine, 5,* 176-190.

Menninger, W.C. (1950). How community forces affect the family. *Bulletin of the Menninger Clinic, 14,* 53-60.

Marmor, J., Bernard, V., & Ottenberg, P. (1960). Psychodynamics of group opposition of health programs. *American Journal of Orthopsychiatry, 30,* 330-345.

Miller, A.C., Fine, A., Adams-Taylor, S., & Schorr, L.B. (1986). *Monitoring children's health: Key indicators.* Washington, DC: American Public Health Association.

Morrill, R.G. (1978). The future for mental health in primary health care programs. *American Journal of Psychiatry, 135,* 1351-1355.

Morris, J.N. (1975). Primary prevention of heart attack. *Bulletin of the New York Academy of Medicine, 51,* 62-74.

Orlandi, M.A. (1987). Promoting health and preventing disease in health care settings: An analysis of barriers. *Preventive Medicine, 16,* 119-130.

President's Commission on Mental Health. (1978). Report (Vol. 1). Washington, DC: US Government Printing Office.

Rae-Grant, N.I. (1982). The implications of primary prevention for the training of the child psychiatrist. *Journal of the American Academy of Child Psychiatry, 21,* 219-224.

Robins, L.N. (1978). Sturdy childhood predictors of antisocial behavior: Replications from longitudinal studies. *Psychological Medicine, 8,* 611.

Russel, M., and Gruber, M. (1987). Risk assessment in environmental policy making. *Science, 236,* 286-290.

Rutter, M. (1979). Protective factors in children's response to stress and disadvantage. In M.W. Reut & J.E. Rolf (Eds.), *Primary prevention of psychopathology* (Vol. 3). Hanover, NH: New England Press.

Ryder, N.B. (1974). The family in developed countries. *Scientific American, 231* (3).

Schvaneveldt, J.D., & Adams, G.R. (1985). Prevention and the family. Part II. *Journal of Primary Prevention, 5,* 141-144.

Spock, B. (1961). *Baby and child care.* New York: Pocket Books.

Stallybrase, C.O. (1948). Mental health in relation to the family with some reference to the National Health Service Act, 1946. *Public Health, 61,* 123-128.

Stone, N.W., Pendleton, V.M., Vaill, M.B., et al. (1982). Primary prevention in mental health: A Head Start demonstration model. *American Journal of Orthopsychiatry, 52,* 360-363.

Tolsma, D.J. (1983). Disease prevention: A societal imperative. *Connecticut Health Bulletin, 97,* 284-288.

Weissman, M.M. (1987). Advances in psychiatric epidemiology: Rates and risks for major depression. *American Journal of Public Health, 77,* 446-451.

World Almanac. (1986). New York: Newspaper Association.

Wynne, L.C., Toohey, M., & Doane, J. (1979). Family studies. In L. Bellak (Ed.), *Disorders of the schizophrenic syndrome.* New York: Basic Books.

Zelnick, M., & Kim, Y. (1982). Sex education and its association with teenage sexual activity, pregnancy and contraceptive use. *Family Planning Perspectives, 14,* 117-126.

2

THE FAMILY AS A SYSTEM

We must first consider an overview of family functioning and construct a framework for frontline professionals through which to assess family performance and discern risks for maldevelopments to an individual or the family as a whole. It must be appreciated that changes in one element of a system reverberate throughout that system, and that any change, positive or negative, in one sector may have beneficial or adverse effects in others.

Universally a family consists of at least two generations. The child's early human environment is almost always the child's biological family, usually with two parents, but it may be a single parent or an extended or substitute family. Single parents, particularly if they are unsupported by other adults and live alone with their offspring, are often handicapped in parental task performance because of the burden of too many role demands. Single parentage can be one of the earliest risk factors predisposing to later troubles. Younger teenage parents, whether single or married, are on the whole at risk for more pregnancy pathology and for parenting deficiencies. An extended family may have advantages or disadvantages as an early environment for the child depending on such specific circumstances as whether familial leadership is clearly defined. Adoptive or foster parents are prone to wonder about a baby's biological background if things do not go well, and such a family lives with a child who may feel that he or she has been rejected at least once.

The prolonged dependency of the human being makes families necessary; ours is the species that is most dependent on others at birth and that remains so the longest. The dependency of the young human being is not only greater and more sustained than that of other mammals but also qualitatively different. Human infants not only grow physically through family care, but need family inputs for the development of their cognitive capacities, for learning how to relate to others and how to employ the symbols and tools of the culture in which they live—characteristics that distinguish humans from all other organisms. The development of mental capacities depends on symbolic operations whose acquisition, in turn, depends on the family's teaching its language, long before formal schooling begins. Thus, family heritage is dual: biological and sociocultural. All societies expect families or substitute agencies to prepare children to become people who can participate in the life of the community and fulfill the adult roles society assigns them or expects from them.

A five-pronged systems view of the family is offered. The following features in the family should be specifically considered in assessing a family's potential success in preparing children for adulthood: 1) leadership, 2) boundaries, 3) emotional climate, 4) communication, and 5) the establishment and accomplishment of goals and tasks through the life cycle stages. Such a family-focused evaluation serves to identify stage-typical risk conditions which can be monitored, ameliorated or corrected through remedial measures. Because the natural developmental tasks for the family as a group and the individuals in it are continuous and also entail different functions from stage to stage, the potential for maldevelopments is recurrent.

LEADERSHIP

Leadership in the family is usually vested in the biological or adoptive parent or parents who serve as models. In cultures like the United States, where children often have limited opportunity to be closely in contact with grandparents or other relatives, the parent(s) may represent the only significant and closely related adults for the young child. The parental model, however, is determined not only by each parent's personality, but also by the relationship between the spouses, the presence or absence of mutual support and esteem, the effectiveness of their communication, and their ways of relating to relatives and others in the community. Power and discipline are important components of leadership in the family. Parental correction should be appropriate to the misdeed, and should not subserve parental hostility or power needs.

Identifiable risks include deviant parental personalities, which may interfere with a marital bond suited to effective parenthood, and social isolation of the couple or parent for various reasons. Parental self-esteem and leadership can also be undermined by chronic parental ill health or economic hardships.

BOUNDARIES

Family boundaries include the individuals' self-boundaries, the boundaries between the generations, and the boundaries between the family and the community. In human systems, boundaries need to be semipermeable; they provide a sense of self or unity for the group, but also enable people to make contact and connection with others outside the family. Self- or ego boundaries are essential for family members' individuality and personhood. The generational boundary distinguishes the parents, as leaders and teachers, and the children, as learners and followers. This boundary is also a barrier across which sexual activity is taboo. The family boundary sets the family apart from the surrounding community; it is usually a living-space boundary which is important in developing a sense of family belonging. This family/community boundary needs to become increasingly permeable; as children grow they need to cross it more freely to participate in the community. Boundaries that are inadequate, overly rigid or overly loose are risks, for they interfere with wholesome family functioning as an open system.

EMOTIONAL CLIMATE

Emotional forces are the glue that holds the family together, especially when the family is not an essential economic unit and when tradition or religion does not rule that the family is indissoluble. No family can function well unless its members care for and support each other. The family needs to be a place where both intimacy and hostility can be tolerated to a greater extent than in the community at large, and where people can relax more freely than they can outside the home.

Discipline and how parents exercise their power are related to, and often determine, the emotional climate of the family. There are also wide cultural variations in emotionality and its expressions. However, if family tradition makes the family out of step with the community in which it lives, risk factors can develop. Symptoms of emotional disturbance in the system require intervention. Serious risks include scapegoating of one family member and child neglect or abuse in any form.

COMMUNICATION

Language, the basis for social interaction, is learned in the family. Language develops best when the child is talked, read and sung to and encouraged to respond to others and express feelings and experiences verbally. Communication consonant with the thinking and values of the community and culture underlies the development of category formation, symbolic processes, and cognition. Any communication handicap is a potential risk factor, and communication difficulties and deviance are significant risk indicators in children's development. Early identification of hearing or visual deficits that interfere with language development and reading are prime responsibilities of parents and frontline caretakers.

FAMILY GOALS AND TASKS

The understanding of family goals and tasks throughout the life cycle is the most important of the five systems components for risk-reducing interventions. Societies expect families to nurture and socialize the young so that they can become full-fledged members of that society who will participate in the work of the community, who will be self-sufficient according to the culture's expectation, and who will reproduce, thus passing on the group's biologic and cultural heritage.

The family life cycle begins with marriage and family formation and passes through many stages as children grow and develop. Even after children emancipate from the family and if the parents live by themselves, the issues of midlife and old age become of concern to both generations, and even to grandchildren.

SUMMARY

Table 3 and Figure 1 summarize the roles and characteristics of the family in human development according to life cycle stages. Listed are some typical, but by no means all, stage-related risks.

Identifying risks depends on understanding family functioning during the various stages and on clinical proficiency in perceiving significant deviations from the normative spectrum, while also being cognizant of sociocultural variations. Identifying family malfunctioning early in the life cycle increases the opportunity for preventive intervention. Statistical evidence of the effectiveness of preventive interventions such as the Head Start program, support programs for unmarried mothers, prenatal care and so forth is available (Stone et al., 1982; Zelnick & Kim, 1982). Clinical wisdom and experience also indicate opportunities to reduce the risks for emotional and psychological disorders in our population.

Preventive interventions by frontline professionals concern risk identification in obviously malfunctioning or disturbed families as well as in families that function well. These tasks involve issues of basic family supports as spelled out by the Family Task Panel of the 1978 Presidential Commission on Mental Health.

Lastly, it is important to remain aware that risk reduction or elimination does not confer immunity for life. Nor is risk identification to be equated with the certain development of mental

TABLE 3
Outline of Family Life Stages

Stage	Biological	Family	Social	Risks
Marriage	Sexual adjustment	Transitions from courtship to planning offspring	New unit and social network; complementary role	Failure to form coalition and social network as a pair
Pre- & neonatal	Helplessness of infant	Start parenthood	Bonding & stimulation	Birth defects, early separation
Infancy	Organization & integration of body systems	Nurturance & weaning	Stimulation & protection	Weaning and nursing problems, under- or overstimulation
Toddler	Motor integration, including language & sphincter mastery, body awareness	Separation; learning behavior controls	Negativism, motoric independence	Overinfantilization, neglectful supervision
Preschool	Body control & mastery	Relationship-ordering, verbal expression of feelings	Language, peer interaction	Language limited to instrumental use, boundary failures, continued erotic attachment to one parent (overly close)

Stage				
Grade school	Smooth body skills & motor coordination	Optimal functioning, unity & harmony	Increased peer network, school & playground	Unity failures, school phobias, isolation, peer problems
Puberty & adolescence	Growth spurt, sexual maturation, motor discoordination & renewed body mastery	Experiments with independence; reconcile communication with need for privacy	Peer relationships more intense than family	Adverse peer influence, lack of parental tolerance for separation
Emancipation	Full growth	Emotional & physical separation	Community partici-pation in school/work	Holding on or extruding; premature assumption of family responsibilities
Early adulthood	Health, pregnancy	New family formation, parenting	Career initiation(s), work	Career problems, failure to consolidate self, lack of intimacy
Midlife	Beginning decline in energy; menopause	Readjustments to dyadic living, grandparenting	Increased social network, participation, retirement	"Empty nest," marital maladjustment
Aging	Facing and coping with more chronic illness or disability—"three leg stage"	Dyadic living, or adjustment to widow-hood, possible leader-ship reversal with children, reminiscing	"Elder status," losses in social field, disengage-ments	Isolation, dependence, unresolved mourning of losses, major life changes (e.g., moving)
Dying	Helplessness, illness	Face dying as a unit, anticipatory mourning	Network support essential	Abandonment of dying member, failure to mourn

Figure 1

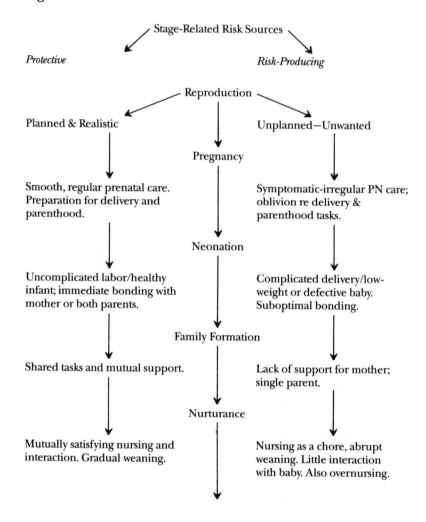

Stage-Related Risk Sources

Protective   *Risk-Producing*

Reproduction

Planned & Realistic   Unplanned—Unwanted

Pregnancy

Smooth, regular prenatal care.   Symptomatic-irregular PN care;
Preparation for delivery and   oblivion re delivery &
parenthood.   parenthood tasks.

Neonation

Uncomplicated labor/healthy   Complicated delivery/low-
infant; immediate bonding with   weight or defective baby.
mother or both parents.   Suboptimal bonding.

Family Formation

Shared tasks and mutual support.   Lack of support for mother;
                                                           single parent.

Nurturance

Mutually satisfying nursing and   Nursing as a chore, abrupt
interaction. Gradual weaning.   weaning. Little interaction
                                                           with baby. Also overnursing.

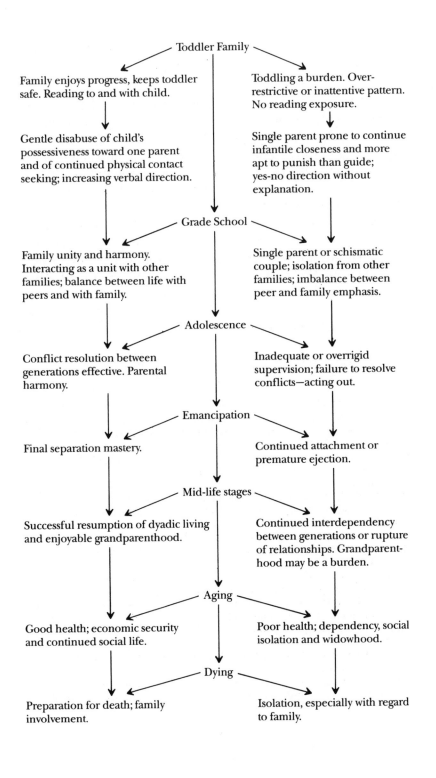

Toddler Family

Family enjoys progress, keeps toddler safe. Reading to and with child.

Toddling a burden. Over-restrictive or inattentive pattern. No reading exposure.

Gentle disabuse of child's possessiveness toward one parent and of continued physical contact seeking; increasing verbal direction.

Single parent prone to continue infantile closeness and more apt to punish than guide; yes-no direction without explanation.

Grade School

Family unity and harmony. Interacting as a unit with other families; balance between life with peers and with family.

Single parent or schismatic couple; isolation from other families; imbalance between peer and family emphasis.

Adolescence

Conflict resolution between generations effective. Parental harmony.

Inadequate or overrigid supervision; failure to resolve conflicts—acting out.

Emancipation

Final separation mastery.

Continued attachment or premature ejection.

Mid-life stages

Successful resumption of dyadic living and enjoyable grandparenthood.

Continued interdependency between generations or rupture of relationships. Grandparent-hood may be a burden.

Aging

Good health; economic security and continued social life.

Poor health; dependency, social isolation and widowhood.

Dying

Preparation for death; family involvement.

Isolation, especially with regard to family.

illness. Children growing up in some very disturbed families may become healthy adults; the reverse can also occur. Community support systems play an important role in alleviating or compensating for family deficiencies and in crises. Foremost among such agencies may be the clergy. Religion, faith, prayer and meditation are support sources for many people. Cultural rites, including funerals, are also important.

Whatever type of intervention may be suitable, reduction or elimination of risks can be effective even if not a guarantee for permanent health. Life events and vicissitudes are complex and unpredictable. We must content ourselves with relative effectiveness of prevention. Much pathology can be forestalled, some cannot, and sometimes resistance to or indifference toward preventive recommendations cannot be overcome.

REFERENCES

Doane, J.A. (1978) Family interaction and communication deviance in disturbed and normal families: A review of research. *Family Process, 17,* 357-376.

Dohler, B., & Grunebaum, H.S. (1980). *Mothers, grandmothers and daughters: Personality and child care in three generation families.* New York: Wiley.

Erickson, E.H. (1982). *The life cycle completed.* New York: W. W. Norton.

Family Service of America. (1984). *The state of families 1984-1985.* New York: Author.

Fleck, S. (1983). Evaluation of the family in general medical care. In H. Leigh (Ed.), *Psychiatry in the practice of medicine.* New York: Addison-Wesley.

Fleck, S. (1984). The family and psychiatry. In B. Saddock & H. Kaplan (Eds.), *Comprehensive textbook of psychiatry* (Vol. 4). Baltimore: Williams & Wilkins.

Herman, J.L. (1981). *Father-daughter incest.* Cambridge, MA: Harvard University Press.

Holmes, S.J., & Robbins, L.N. (1988). The role of parental disciplinary practices in the development of depression and alcoholism. *Psychiatry, 51,* 24-35.

Holmes, T.H., & Masuda, M. (1974). Life change and illness susceptibility. In B.S. Dohrenwend & B.P. Dohrenwend (Eds.), *Stressful life events.* New York: Wiley.

Horner, M., Nadelson, C., & Notman, M. (Eds.) (1983). *The challenge of change: Perspectives on family, work and education.* New York: Plenum Press.

Huygen, F.J.A. (1982). *Family medicine: The medical life histories of families.* New York: Brunner/Mazel.

Kellam, S.G., Ensminger, M.E., & Turner, R.S. (1977). Family structure and the mental health of children. *Archives of General Psychiatry, 34,* 1012-1022.

Leehan, J., & Wilson, L.P. (1985). *Grown-up abused children.* Springfield, IL: C C Thomas.

Lewis, J.M., Beavers, W.R., Gossett, J.T., & Phillips, V.A. (1976). *No single thread: Psychological health in family systems.* New York: Brunner/Mazel.

Litman, T.J. (1974). The family as a basic unit in health and medical care: A social-behavioral overview. *Social Science Medicine, 8,* 495–519.

Miller, J.G., & Miller, J.L. (1980). The family as a system: In C.K. Hofling & J.M. Lewis (Eds.), *The family: Evaluation and treatment* (pp. 141–184). New York: Brunner/Mazel.

Smilkstein, G. (1979). *Instructions for use of the family APGAR: A family function screening questionnaire.* Seattle: Department of Family Medicine, University of Washington.

Smith, R.M., & Smith, C.W. (1981). Child rearing and single-parent fathers. *Family Relations, 30,* 411–417.

Solnit, A.J. (1980). The appraisal of the individual in the family: Criteria for healthy psychological development in childhood. In C.K. Hofling & J.M. Lewis (Eds.), *Family evaluation and treatment* (pp. 71–85). New York: Brunner/Mazel.

Stone, N.W., Pendleton, V.M., Vaill, M.B., et al. (1982). Primary prevention in mental health: A Head Start demonstration model. *American Journal of Orthopsychiatry, 52,* 360–363.

Winnicott, D.W. (1965). *The maturational processes and the facilitating environment.* New York: International Universities Press.

Zelnick, M., & Kim, Y. (1982). Sex education and its association with teenage sexual activity, pregnancy and contraceptive use. *Family Planning Perspectives, 14,* 117–126.

Zuravin, S.J. (1987). Unplanned pregnancies, family planning problems, and child maltreatment. *Family Relations, 36,* 135–139.

3

MARRIAGE AND FAMILY FORMATION

Mrs. A, a 27-year-old wife and secretary in the fourth month of her uneventful first pregnancy, appeared sad and preoccupied to the obstetrical nurse-clinician. Upon inquiry, Mrs. A said that her husband seemed to lack "a sense of family," that he seemed less and less interested in her although he had attended prenatal instruction sessions regularly. The nurse felt puzzled by this complaint for she knew that the pregnancy had been planned and decided upon by both of them.

The nurse learned that the husband had been coming home later and later, claiming that he was busy with extra work because of an impending promotion which entailed a transfer to a city about a thousand miles away. The patient complained further that he had stopped working on the half-finished house that they had mostly built themselves and that he no longer went with her on the weekend trips to their respective families, who lived only 50 miles away. The couple had done this regularly over the five years of their marriage; they spent every weekend with either set of parents, but always saw hers at least briefly. The nurse-clinician learned that this couple had no social life as a couple. They each had their own circle of friends, but had spent all their weekends either working on their house or with their families. Mr. and Mrs. A got along well enough in their marriage and were sexually compatible. The patient's complaint that her husband lacked "respect for family" referred more to the possibility of Mrs. A having to separate from her parents than to any concern about motherhood and their becoming a family with a baby. The nurse-clinician suggested that Mr. and Mrs. A come in together for a session, but he refused, claiming he had to spend more

and more time away in preparation for his likely transfer.
However, Mr. A continued to attend the prenatal classes faithfully.

This vignette illustrates some of the important tasks of marriage
and the prenatal period. In modern societies, marital partners are
usually expected not only to live apart from their families of origin,
but also to become emotionally independent of their parents.
Another task is to evolve friendships and a social network as a
couple, besides working on their mutual relationship in the everyday give-and-take of life. Although Mr. and Mrs. A shared meals
and economic existence, they had failed to establish a mutual
relationship and continued to live like single friends who were
together primarily for the sake of sexual intimacy. While they were
prepared and eager to function as parents, they had not faced the
task of emancipating themselves from their respective parental
origins. The threat of living apart from their families, and particularly from her family, precipitated the current crisis and mood
change in this prospective mother, raising the risk of depression,
especially during the postpartum period.

Heterosexual human pairing and monogamy existed prehistor-
ically as did polygamy and, rarely, polyandry. When marriage
became a recognized and formal institution is unknown, but family
formation is thousands of years old. Marriage existed when nomadic
life was the rule, but became an economic and social necessity
when people settled down and became agricultural. Spouses did
not necessarily live together, as they still do not in some New
Guinea societies. In most societies, and certainly in modern societies,
the underlying bases of marriage are mixed: sexual, reproductive,
social and economic. Bacon pointed out that neither the man who
marries solely for money nor the man who marries solely for love
has his wits about him.

In Western societies, the history of marriage is also mixed. In the
past Western marriages were based on interfamilial arrangements,
at least among the affluent, and more recently increasingly on
"being in love." In most societies now individuals choose for them-

selves and do so based on the belief that they are in love. Not infrequently marriage occurs because an unintended pregnancy has occurred. A marriage so begun is at risk for failure, especially from the mental health standpoint, even if separation or divorce does not follow.

The mutual attraction usually involves conscious and unconscious elements in each partner. Outsiders often can recognize that a chosen partner shows similarities to a parent or sibling, but the prospective marital partners may be unaware of such similarities. From the mental health standpoint, the central feature of marriage is mutual commitment regardless of the intensity or lack of mutual attraction. Historically there is no evidence that arranged marriages are any less successful and effective in the long run than are partnerships based on mutual affection. Of prime importance is that the mutual commitment made by prospective partners be based on some awareness of the human life cycle, and the marital and family life cycles in particular. Spouses need to expect and accept that their relationship will change over time, hoping that it will become more intimate and mutually satisfying. Their partnership also needs to be resilient in the face of expectable and unforeseeable pressures and crises. These are usually intimated in the marital vows "for better or worse, in sickness and in health."

Newlyweds must appreciate that living and growing together does not just mean "playing house." They need to adjust to each other's foibles and either change them or accept them, whether they are a failure to put the cap on the toothpaste, different tastes in food and entertainment, or different sleep and wake cycles. If partners are committed to each other, they can evolve effective mutuality, nurture each other, help each other grow, and care for and respect each other.

Marriage can be a boon to the mental and emotional health of each partner. But it can also be a detriment for individuals who may find intimacy threatening, who lack the capacity to sustain a commitment, or who find themselves disappointed because of unforeseen personality foibles, be they pathology in the spouse, value conflicts or other incompatibilities.

In Western societies, where sexuality is still a facet of the human condition beset by much ambivalence, sexual difficulties and conflicts may arise because of inhibitions in either partner or both. It is often assumed by young people that once a person is sexually mature physiologically, intercourse becomes a matter of course, without any realization that partners need to learn how to adjust to and please one another. The ability to communicate about sexual matters is important and is often lacking. Included in such communication should be a mutual understanding and agreement about contraception, because adjustment to married life should take precedence over reproduction. Religions that emphasize the primacy of procreation are in conflict with sound principles of achieving unity as a couple before becoming a threesome. It is preferable that the first pregnancy be postponed until the spouses have established their own intimate relationship and also have begun to form a social network as a couple. This is especially important if the couple live at some distance from their respective families of origin, for it is after childbirth or in other crises that help can come from friends, aside from that of professionals. Young families benefit from associating with other young families for their own companionship, for the opportunity to talk about common problems or concerns and, eventually, for the possible companionship of their offspring.

Currently marriage as an institution is considered to be in crisis because of the high divorce rate (especially in the United States), because of a preference for living together without the formality of marriage, and because of the high incidence of single parenthood. These variations from the presumed traditional marriage and family formation may constitute risks for mental health impairment, but they are not in and of themselves indications of illness or of familial pathology. Single parenthood has always been a common condition, in the past due to widowhood more often than now. As indicated, single parenthood is not pathological in itself, although it carries certain risks. Children need more than one parental figure. Preferably they need one of each sex. Although substitute parental figures are often available—the mother's boyfriend, grandparents, an uncle or aunt, a teacher—isolated single parenthood is a risk to the family's mental health.

Making deliberate decisions about family formation (or addition) is most important for newlyweds or longer wedded couples. Unfortunately, and particularly disadvantageous from the mental health vantage point, this step is often not one of conscious joint deliberation and decision. Whether married or unmarried, people from the early teenage years on often reproduce without much consideration of the future. They may want children—"a baby so I have something of my own" in the case of some deprived teenagers or "a baby for him" in some cultures—without the awareness that babyhood is brief and childhood long. Such parents often are unprepared even for the toddler stage.

RISKS

Lacking preparation or the personal capacities and maturity for parenthood constitutes a major, and maybe the most important, risk for the mental health of parents, of children, and of the family as a unit. If children are wanted, but the timing or socioeconomic conditions are not what parents had planned for their first pregnancy, there are nine months to reconcile earlier plans before the reality of becoming a threesome. Prenatal programs can be helpful for couples or single mothers in preparing for parenthood, including those who may ultimately choose to terminate an unplanned pregnancy, possibly because tests revealed fetal abnormalities. Although the decision to abort is always difficult and fraught with emotion, many women consider it a more responsible and ethical act than beginning (or adding to) their parenthood before they are ready.

Involuntary infertility is also a rather common source of distress. If one partner is found to be the "cause" of this condition, that partner is likely to feel guilty and somehow like less than a full person. Usually efforts to adopt a baby ensue. The adoption process is a stressful experience at best, and one that has become more difficult and uncertain as the number of available babies dwindles. Laws usually require adoption through an agency, which "evaluates" the prospective parents, something never done for natural parents. Even if adoption approval is obtained, a long wait and often considerable expense lie ahead. All of these conditions produce mental health risks for the parents-to-be and possibly for the adoptee as well. However, many patterns of adoption practice are currently changing. "Independent" (i.e., nonagency) adoptions through intermediaries such as attorneys and physicians, as well as through advertisements by those who seek to adopt, are increasing. There is also greater readiness for cross-cultural and cross-racial adoptions and for the adoption of older children. Another route to parenthood is that of surrogate motherhood, but this method can become a source of stress, pain and intense conflict for all concerned.

Divorce bespeaks lack of commitment as often as it is the result of unforeseeable incompatibilities. However, the increment in the divorce rate over the last 50 years takes on different meaning when we realize that the average lifespan of marriages has almost doubled during this century. Therefore, unresolved conflicts or incompatibilities that a century ago would often have been ended by the death of one of the partners now can last and fester a much longer period of time. Also, runaway spouses were more common 100 years ago than now. Furthermore, divorce has become a much easier way of resolving marital conflicts than it was 50 years ago. Cross-sectional statistics such as "there is one divorce for every two marriages" are misleading because the majority of marriages last as they "always" have. When divorce was difficult to implement due to cultural, legal, religious or economic reasons, spouses may have continued to live together unhappily in chronic strife and conflict. Some still do.

Divorce can be a constructive solution for the marital partners. It is never entirely constructive for all family members. Separating partners are usually put at a considerable economic disadvantage, and the noncustodial parent rarely finds it possible to function as a parent over time even if strongly motivated to do so. The mental health decrements for the children of divorced parents—even if children can recognize that the divorce was necessary—have been studied thoroughly in recent years (Wallerstein & Kelly, 1980) and are now well known. Children may be better off after a divorce in some instances and can also benefit by mastering pain and distress.

Widowhood and widowerhood are also burdensome for families, for the surviving partner and the children, although there is less conflict than is likely after a divorce. Often there are economic problems as well, especially for divorcees. Many widows and divorcees also find themselves quickly disconnected from their regular social networks, and sometimes are viewed by their female friends as potential competitors and by men as readily available. Thus, even if these women seek another marriage, maybe a better one than their previous experience, unmarried men are not rushing in to take on the duties of stepparenthood.

Divorced parents are more prepared to meld their families; unfortunately this often occurs without adequate preparation for the difficulties that such cross-stepparenting entails. Such reconstructed families usually have to bridge more life cycle stages than original families need to, and the new couple may also decide to have offspring together—an event rarely welcomed by older half-siblings. Thus, reconstituted families harbor risks for unhappiness, conflicts and pathological jealousies, but again risks which need not result in pathological developments. Special counseling or family therapy can alleviate these expectable risks before jealousies and conflicts become chronic and evolve into mental disorders.

Pathological marriages often result in spouse abuse. Although it is generally assumed that spouse battering is mostly wife battering, actually it is close to 50/50. The difference is that men are usually stronger, apt to do more damage, and use weapons much more frequently. Child abuse is even more common than spouse abuse, and violence in the family unfortunately is a serious but insufficiently recognized problem. Most assaultive criminals have grown up in violent families. Family violence occurring in at least 20% of United States families is habitual and rarely becomes available for remedial measures until injuries bring the abused member to medical attention. Even then, a wife who has been battered often withdraws formal charges when her husband pleads with her, often blaming alcohol and promising change (Gelles, 1979, 1987).

PREVENTIVE INTERVENTIONS

Preventive measures begin with premarital counseling, a requirement in many religious institutions before the marriage ceremony can be performed. In addition to private practitioners, in most communities there are agencies that provide premarital and marital counseling. However, the most important health-promoting, if not preventive, programs are those of family life and sex education, which should be offered in all schools beginning in early grades (Marsiglio & Mott, 1986). Such instruction—including information about sexuality and contraception, the family life cycle, and parenthood responsibilities—is essential and effective in terms of reducing the number of undesired pregnancies, teenage pregnancies in particular. An increase in the number of young people who use contraception after such courses has been demonstrated (Zelnick & Kim, 1982). The difficulties of, and impediments to, instituting such risk-reducing programs were discussed in the Introduction.

The first pregnancy and related instruction about delivery and infant care are another opportunity for family life education, especially if partners attend these programs together. As in the vignette beginning this chapter, this is what happened once the nurse pointed out that Mrs. A recognized that she was distraught over the impending separation from her parents and that this emancipatory step was long overdue. Mr. and Mrs. A could then discuss these problems on their own; they resolved to start weaning themselves from their tangible closeness to their parents. The weekend routine was changed, and they began to spend time with friends made in their prenatal class. The delivery and postnatal period were uneventful, and a few months after, they moved happily, appreciating each other and their baby, and both enjoying the rewards of the husband's success.

The nurse's effective intervention required her not only to listen patiently to Mrs. A but also to know what to listen for, recognizing the psychological and emotional territory of a first-time mother-to-be. The nurse practitioner knew that pregnant women often seek renewed closeness to their own mothers and understood that Mrs. A's complaint that "he lacks a sense of family" referred to her parents and not the family they were about to create.

REFERENCES

Beavers, R.W. (1985). *Successful marriage: A family system approach to couples therapy.* New York: W.W. Norton.

Bernard, V.W. (1974). Adoption. In S. Arieti (Ed.), *American handbook of psychiatry* (Vol. 1, 2nd ed.). New York: Basic Books.

Bibring, G., & Valenstein, A. (1976). Psychological aspects of pregnancy. *Clinical Obstetrics and Gynecology, 19,* 357–371.

Blake, J. (1974). The changing status of women in developed countries. *Scientific American, 231.*

Bohman, M. (1971). A study of adopted children, their background, environment and adjustment. *Acta Paediatrica Scandinavica, 61,* 90–97.

Cramer, S.H., Keitel, M.H., & Rossberg, R.H. (1986). The family and employed mothers. *International Journal of Family Psychiatry, 7,* 17–34.

Dunbar, C., Edwards, V., Gede, E., et al. (1979). Successful coping styles in professional women. *Canadian Journal of Psychiatry, 24,* 43–46.

Finkelhor, D. (1986). *A source book on child sexual abuse.* Beverly Hills, CA: Sage.

Gelles, R.T. (1979). *Family violence.* London: Sage.

Gelles, R.T. (1987). The family and its role in the abuse of children. *Psychiatric Annals, 17,* 299–232.

Gray, E.B. (1982). Prenatal support programs: A strategy for the primary prevention of child abuse. *Journal of Primary Prevention, 2,* 138–152.

Litman, T.J. (1974). The family as a basic unit in health and medical care: A social-behavioral overview. *Social Science and Medicine, 8,* 495–519.

Marsiglio, W., & Mott, F. L. (1986). The impact of sex education on sexual activity, contraceptive use and premarital pregnancy among American teenagers. *Family Planning Perspectives, 18,* 151–170.

Notman, M., & Nadelson, C. (1981). Changing views of femininity and childbearing. *Hillside Journal of Clinical Psychiatry, 3,* 187–202.

Rossi, A. (1968). Transition to parenthood. *Journal of Marriage and the Family, 30,* 26–39.

Visher, E., & Visher, J. (1982). *How to win as a stepparent.* New York: W.W. Norton.

Wallerstein, J.S., & Kelly, J.B. (1980). *Surviving the breakup: How children and parents cope with divorce.* New York: Basic Books.

Zelnick, M., & Kim, Y. (1982). Sex education and its association with teenage sexual activity, pregnancy and contraception use. *Family Planning Perspectives, 14,* 117–126.

4

THE FIRST YEAR—THE NURTURANT FAMILY

ATTACHMENT REGULATION AND INTEREST IN THE WORLD

Mrs. C seemed tense and awkwardly handled her firstborn, 5-week-old boy, David. She complained about his fussiness and "jittery" mood and had concluded that since nothing she did seemed to calm him down, she wasn't "fit" to be a mother. Most of her attempts at stopping his crying centered around stimulating toys and games "to get his attention." This seemed to make him more irritable, and she found little satisfaction in caring for him. David's feeding and sleeping cycles were quite irregular, and Mrs. C compared them unfavorably to those of her friend's more phlegmatic child.

To make matters worse, Mrs. C had asked her mother to stay on to "teach me how to care for him," but her mother was becoming "bossy" and conflict was developing about how to care for David. Mrs. C's question for the doctor was whether it would hurt a child for the mother to return to work early —"Maybe for my sanity I should go back to work now."

Mr. C was spending extra time at work competing for a promotion and felt himself at a loss as to how to help his wife calm his son.

Dr. A found that David was physically normal, but thought that food allergies might be a part of the problem. She instructed Mrs. C to change the baby's formula. She also tried to increase Mrs. C's self-confidence by citing examples of other mothers who had difficulty with their first child: "Don't worry, the strangeness will wear off and you'll feel more comfortable as time goes on." However, Dr. A wanted to learn more about the family situation, as the mother's wish to return to work now might be due to her desire to evade the problems at home.

The first task of the newborn is to stabilize and become regulated in reacting to internal and external stimulations. Infants are capable of perceiving and responding to sounds, sights, touch, smells, and their own and others' movements. The next step for the infant is to elicit pleasurable experiences so as to fall in love with the human world, while establishing a primary attachment to the main nurturer. The third achievement during the first year consists of using this pleasure in the surrounding world to communicate with others in a purposeful manner to make things happen—to be fed, to be played with, or to have diapers changed.

The adaptive tasks of the first year of life concern the range of emotions or emotional themes that are organized: Can babies, as they are learning to communicate, show dependency by reaching out to be picked up? Do they explore by examining mommy's nose or mouth? Can they communicate protest or anger by looking daddy in the eye or throwing food on the floor? During the first months of life, the family members, including siblings, besides being comforting and protective, can stimulate. They can reach out, seducing the baby into finding the human world pleasurable, and the family can learn to "read" rather than anticipate the baby's signals, and can respond in an active and pleasurable way, thus helping the baby to differentiate between dependency gestures and aggressive or assertive outreach.

The differential reading of signals in an empathic way, along with wooing the baby, appealing to the baby's senses, and providing comfort and security, are the main family tasks. All members contribute to this and thereby help broaden the range of excitation and stimulation. Fathers are usually more action oriented and mothers more responsive to fine motor development. Siblings may appeal to the baby's vision and spatial sense by playing games that involve movement, while mothers encourage reciprocal vocalizations. While in the first few months of life the achievement of homeostasis is essential, over the next several months higher levels of organization appear.

Having achieved some capacity for self-regulation and for engaging the world, the infant becomes selectively interested in the human world, more selective in interpersonal interaction, and better able to form a special relationship with the primary caregiver. Babies are born with different temperaments, and newborns react differently, thus requiring different responses—maybe more attention, maybe less. Such differences are not abnormal or a risk condition unless the family fails to adjust and adapt accordingly. The development of nonverbal communications parallels the gradual development of recognizing basic schemes of causality—means to ends, connections which, together with the basic capacity for human attachment, are a requisite for, and a precursor to, the later development of a healthy sense of self.

Risks

Infants who cannot maintain an equilibrium in the face of internal and external stimulation may become very fussy and upset when hungry or being held, and may not seek out further stimulation. Indeed, they may shut out stimuli that disrupt their equilibrium. Alternatively, they may become labile, hyperreactive and unfocused in attempts to maintain contact with the environment. Such hyper- and hyporeactive infants have a very difficult time establishing physiological rhythms and fail to achieve homeostasis. They are at risk for further maldevelopments.

Successful growth and development depend on the infant's capacities and on those of the supporting family members. The unresponsive environment fails to support and can even undermine homeostatic capacities. The unavailable or inconsistent caregiver does not offer physical comfort or a sense of security. A caretaker's unpredictability may destabilize the infant's emerging cycles and patterns instead of promoting stabilization by comforting engagement. The dangerous or abusive caretaker threatens the physical integrity of the infant. Hypo- or hyperstimulating or dull caretakers may compromise an infant's own tendency to engage the world, leaving the baby apathetic, withdrawn or hyperreactive.

Clinicians can observe increases in infants' capacities to organize, regulate and console themselves, to find the world interesting, and to interact with it even during the first month of life. Developmental lags or regressions in these capacities can be observed. At the worst level, the deficient family fails to provide physical care, adequate nutrition and protection, does not respond to illness, pain or distress, or is physically abusive.

At subtler levels, however, adverse infant care must be assessed in terms of the parent's ability to respond empathically and comfort the baby, which is basic for human attachment. Are the parents available, and do they help the infants to build on their innate capacities for comfort and regulation by touching, holding, rocking, looking at, and talking to the baby? Depressed or withdrawn mothers, or immature or self-centered ones, may be able to care for babies' physical needs, feeding them adequately and taking them for medical attention when they are ill. These same mothers, however, may be so self-absorbed that they cannot provide the comforting and engaging functions so essential to human development.

There may also be deficits in the mothers' capacity to "read" the babies' fundamental cues with respect to pleasure and pain. Psychotic mothers responding to their own delusions or inner voices, or severely depressed and self-absorbed mothers, may not read the infants' distress signals. Such mothers may not be able to observe or grasp when an infant is alert and ready to be engaged, and thus may not offer appropriate comforting, protecting or stimulation. Mothers who are unusually angry or ambivalent may feel overwhelmed, especially if single and living alone. Such disadvantaged mothers may communicate their dissatisfaction or mixed feelings to their infants; they may hold and feed the baby, but with a wooden body posture, tense facial expressions, jerky rather than rhythmic handling, and harsh voices or looks. A mother might concentrate on a television program while mechanically tending to the infant. Conversely, an overactive family may overwhelm and confuse the infant, who may either remain labile and chaotic in responding, or even withdraw.

Beyond Risks

The most severe attachment disorder appears in autistic infants who, because of genetic or constitutional difficulties, never fully achieve homeostasis and therefore do not move on to the task of human attachment. The infant whose constitutional differences make physical touch or other kinds of human stimulation painful may also have a proclivity for attachment disorder. Infantile depression, psychophysiological disorders (vomiting or colic), failure to thrive, and feeding and sleep disturbances may all be related to profound attachment failure. Infants with severe allergies or celiac disease are also at risk for attachment failures.

The capacity for attachment can be assessed through the degree of relatedness and synchrony: how the infant and mother respond to each other. Adaptive infants can recognize and respond to a wide range of cues and are able to recover from a momentary disappointment when their signals are not met. Thus, when a mother is preoccupied, a healthy baby can recapture her attention by smiling, reaching out or making appealing sounds until she finally responds.

In contrast, mothers who misread infants' signals may withdraw at the slightest hint that the baby is not responding. In some instances, infant and mother may be physically in touch and may even have a range of shared affects available to them, yet somehow each member of the pair appears to be out of sync with the other. They do come together, but each one seems preoccupied. Such lack of attachment stems not from an inability to invest themselves in each other, but from the way in which they misread each other's signals—a communication failure.

A maladaptive infant may show only mechanical or intermittent excited responses. Gradations of pleasure do not seem evident. There may be only one type of affect—mild, compliant pleasure, for instance—with no capacity for protest or expression of frustration. Or the baby may only protest, showing little pleasure, and rest and relax only occasionally. Such infants have little capacity to resist stress and are at risk for further developmental lags. David, in the vignette at the beginning of this chapter, is at such risk unless his mother can be helped to become more effectively nurturant, even after some allergy problems may have been identified. Mrs. C needs help to understand her baby's physiological sensitivities and needs, and to recognize that the problems are not evidence of poor mothering. Nurturing and mothering need to be "tailored" for each infant.

Preventive Interventions

Risk-reducing interventions aim at transforming a growth-inhibiting family environment so that it becomes adapted to an infant's individual needs, whether hypo- or hyperreactive. The first step is the assessment of the strengths and vulnerabilities of the newborn infant in terms of the baby's capacity to achieve homeostasis. Impediments to psychophysiological organization and regulation— among them sensory hypersensitivities, immaturity in sensorimotor integration, difficulties in forming regular cycles of alertness and sleep, eating, and so forth—need to be considered. The mother-child interaction must be assessed for possible failures in responding to the infant.

Specific sensitivities or low stimulus thresholds of infants should be identified so that protective measures can be taken. For example, a baby with a tactile or auditory sensitivity should be protected from undue noise and be handled soothingly. Eventually, normal maturation will obviate the necessity for such precautions. Pairing gradual exposure to the noxious stimuli with pleasurable experiences will help youngsters overcome or outgrow particular sensitivities. For example, infants hypersensitive to sound in almost all ranges may be spoken to at the same time as they are soothingly and rhythmically rocked. Thus, the upsetting experience of hearing noise is combined with the soothing experience of being rocked, permitting the child to receive auditory stimulation while achieving modulation and regulation by a complementary, comforting experience.

Of course, this approach can be used with other modalities, and maturation, if not impeded, helps the youngster develop appropriate stimulus thresholds. Sometimes more generalized difficulty in achieving internal regulation calls for a careful assessment of the individual differences in order to find an experience, such as rocking an infant to the rhythm of the mother's heart rate, which is soothing and regulating. Some infants prefer to be held in a special position. One baby might not be ready to be held in a vertical position and may need to spend more time in being held close to the body in a relatively horizontal position, while another may be soothed by being held vertically over the parent's shoulder.

The other primary goal during the stage of homeostasis is to facilitate the infant's engagement in the world. Withdrawn infants who sleep all day do not have an opportunity to become interested in the things around them. Infants with poor muscle tone or severe muscle rigidity will find it difficult to accommodate their body to their mothers', and cannot use body contact optimally for exploring the animate or inanimate world. Initially, the stimulus may have to be made especially interesting for a particular infant. A baby with intact hearing who does not react to sound may first require sounds combined with other sensory experiences such as touch or visual stimulation until the infant will respond to sound alone. The baby whose body becomes rigid and who turns away when held may require exposure to especially comforting and pleasurable physical experiences. These might include being held in certain positions and a combination of being talked to, looked at, held and rocked until relaxation and enjoyable physical comfort are achieved.

Infants with muscular rigidity may require a wide range of motion exercises in which arms and legs are gently moved passively, combined with experiences which tend to soothe and relax the whole body. "Floppy" youngsters with poor muscle tone may improve motor control by means of the extra exercise they get when moving their limbs as part of pleasurable experiences. The movements infants make in response to things they see or hear may appear to be random, but they are often semipurposeful. Rhythmic sing-songs offer infants the opportunity to try to move arms and limbs in a responsive way, thus enhancing control.

Parents of an infant who avoids gaze contact need to be taught how to use new stimuli gradually to engage the baby visually. To this end, various facial expressions, perhaps grimaces, or colorful objects can help to gain the infant's attention and responses.

Babies showing only shallow emotions—weak, transitory smiles, for example—need mothers who can find experiences that provide more intense pleasure and that can be built on systematically in order to deepen the infant's capacity for joy. If an infant's initial attachment lacks stability and is easily disrupted through discomfort or the mother's failure to read cues, the situation, if identified, can easily be remedied. Parents can be taught to seek reengagement with the child, avoiding long periods of nonattachment.

Parents can also be encouraged to help the baby achieve a sense of personal uniqueness by fostering a favored interaction in games and routines. In all these areas, educative advice may suffice so long as the parents learn to interpret the infant's cues and to expand and integrate sensory modalities so as to broaden the baby's range of affects. Parents who are emotionally disturbed because of intrapersonal or interpersonal problems that interfere with attachment may need a more integrated program involving support in addition to education.

In helping parents and other caretakers understand and work through difficulties in the attachment phase, the unique way a particular infant or phase of infant development contributes to maladaptive parental reactions needs to be appreciated. Infants who are overly intense, clinging, withdrawn, labile, excessively irritable, or overly alert may evoke different aspects or parental sensibilities or conflicts. The mother-infant match—or mismatch—is more important than any particular characteristics of either individual. Similarly, the family or extended family may reveal characteristic group patterns that undermine optimal attachment. Parents need to recognize disruptive influences such as a sibling's or spouse's jealously or other disorganization which may have resulted from the infant's entry into the family circle. Finally, it should be noted that external, interpersonal and intrapersonal factors rarely exist in isolation from one another.

When severe stress, illness, poverty, single parenthood, isolation or child abuse interferes with adaptation in this phase, cooperation among health, mental health, social and legal service agencies is critical in providing needed relief and supports. These services can include providing homemakers, surrogate caretakers, psychological help or financial or legal assistance. Programs designed to prevent maladaptive patterns must be able to draw on a wide range of support systems and professionals in order to help the infant and family.

Although David did not suffer from any detectable allergies, the physician's reassurance and suggestions about holding, soothing and more comfortable ways of feeding David helped the mother to feel more competent and in charge. As she calmed down and set a date for her mother's departure, David also became less irritable, and he and his mother began to enjoy each other. Suggestions from the office nurse about how to play with and stimulate David helped Mrs. C a great deal. Appropriate attachment between the two developed, setting the stage for other engagements, including the "introduction" of the father, who felt more at ease after his promotion.

Family functioning improved simultaneously. The leadership confusion and diffusion created by the grandmother/mother-in-law's presence was resolved as Mrs. C began to take charge, supported by both the physician's office staff and then her husband, who in a sense rejoined the family. The climate, which had been tense because of poor communication between mother and child, improved. The task of maintaining and broadening attachments between mother and infant had been threatened, but the risks in this regard were reduced or eliminated with the help of the frontline office staff and the husband's assumption of his paternal role.

LEARNING PURPOSEFUL COMMUNICATION

Jill, age 8 months, was an adorable little girl, smiling, alert and easily soothed. Although physically healthy and closely attached to her mother, Mrs. K, Jill was delayed in her development— barely crawling, vocalizing little, and failing to initiate reciprocal interactive or play. Mrs. K seemed unconcerned with these deficiencies, which were quite apparent to the visiting nurse, and allowed only that "Jill is a little slow and needs more taking care of." The nurse observed that Jill's mother interfered with any move Jill tried to make away from her, even if only to crawl away a few feet and turn to look at her from a little distance. Mother would immediately force Jill back on her shoulder because "she needs to be comforted."

Any attempt to point out to Mrs. K that Jill was ready for "more independence" and needed it were met with a "she needs to be held close" or "she needs to be filled up," a misinterpretation of Jill's every cry as one of hunger. The nurse decided that Mrs. K had personal problems that interfered with her accepting advice, and the staff social worker began to work with her. Jill's father, an alcoholic, refused to participate in any sessions despite repeated invitations to do so.

Once a secure human attachment is achieved through the mutual cueing and reciprocal responses of infant and mother, a process of differentiation should occur in the affective, behavioral and somatic realms of experience. Through this process, basic schemes of causality are established that form the basis for reality testing. Anna Freud's (1966) "body-mind differentiation" refers to the infant's task to transform internal "emotional" sensations into organized psychological or mental representations. Advancement in somatopsychological integration may be observed with the appearance at eight months of what Spitz (1957) called "stranger anxiety." However, social interaction, as well as play with objects, facilitates differentiation. Responsiveness by adults helps infants appreciate that they can initiate interactions. When infants smile and the mother smiles in response, babies begin to realize their creative power. Patterns of cognition and interaction as well as subtle emotional and empathic exchanges evolve in a responsive parent-child interpersonal repertoire. If empathic interaction between parent and infant is lacking because the former responds in a mechanical or remote manner or projects his or her own feelings onto the baby, the infant may not learn to appreciate basic causal relationships, e.g., that one's anger can cause another to feel bad. Such an infant may show gastric distress instead of motor activity when communicating emotional hunger or frustration. There are some infants who are able to assert themselves adequately but who are unable to enjoy relationships with people. Stimulating these developments is the task of the nurturant family, notably that of the mother or her substitute.

Risks

The 8-month-old infant who smiles and looks happy but has no capacity to signal purposefully or who responds to the mother's signals with random or chaotic gestures is displaying a developmental lag and is at risk for further deviance. A less severe problem exists when only one aspect of emotional differentiation is compromised; for example, the baby's anger may be ignored or lead to withdrawal by the parent. Symptoms such as sensorimotor delays, apathy, intense chronic fear (prolonged stranger anxiety), clinging, lack of exploratory activity and curiosity, flat emotional reactions to significant adults, and frequent specific maladaptive behaviors such as biting, chronic crying, and irritability may all represent disorders in somatopsychological differentiation. Constitutional factors or difficulties in the previous stages of homeostasis can hamper optimal development. Problems may also result from the parents' lack of responsiveness or inappropriate responses to the infant's signals—a particular risk for single parents living alone with the baby.

Growth-promoting environments at this stage of development read and respond to the infant's communications at the behavioral, somatic and affective levels. An inhibiting family environment may either not respond at all or may respond only to certain of the infant's signals such as protest or anger, and not to others such as joy or curiosity. An apathetic or indifferent parent may fail to help the infant with the use of new signals or to foster resilience by offering alternatives to meet frustrations. Such failures in infant care and engagement can be observed by frontline practitioners when watching the infant interacting with and responding to others.

Mothers are often concerned at this stage that the infant does not find them "interesting enough." One mother, for example, did not read her infant's signals well largely because they were weak. When her son did not brighten up for her, she assumed that it was she who was uninteresting and unappealing. Another common fear has to do with conflicts of assertion. As infants assert their needs more forcefully, parents often need to respond assertively. Sometimes, however, an adult's assertiveness derives from fear of angry feelings, as in the case of a father who felt the urge to slap his child whenever the child showed any sort of assertive protest. Because of the father's fear of his own angry feelings, he remained passive and unresponsive to the infant.

Preventive Interventions

In correcting an infant's less-than-optimal capacities, the basic principle is to offer repetitive, pleasurable, gradually more interesting and wider-ranging stimuli for the particular underused capacity. For example, where sensorimotor coordination is vulnerable, increasing the range and complexity of stimulation while holding the youngster's attention is in order. The infant who looks but rarely reaches out a hand can be offered a new object as part of the social interchange.

Where a range of ordinarily expectable moods or affects is not present, the principle of intervention is the same. With the infant who cannot show pleasure, different combinations of novel stimuli may evoke a brief smile, if only for a fleeting second or two. That brief smile may then become the basis for further emotional elaboration.

Some infants become disorganized with any social engagement. In such instances, the clinician needs to identify experiences that can help the youngsters focus attention for successively longer periods of time without becoming disorganized. Furthermore, conflicts, character limitations, gross personality disturbances in the mother, or a family disturbance must be considered. The infant's increasing autonomy and demands for clearer communications can place a special burden on the family as a unit. The clinician's understanding of the family's collective affective response in dealing with the infant is a very important component of a successful treatment strategy and may provide risk reduction in subsequent development.

In Jill's case the problems were rooted in Mrs. K's personality problems and a conflicted marriage with an alcoholic husband who unduly depended on her. She was therefore referred to a family service agency. As she became more involved with the social worker, Mrs. K attempted to dominate the sessions and would frequently interrupt the social worker. It was possible to point out the parallel between her interference with the therapist's communication and her interference with her baby's attempts to interact more and in new ways. Then the treatment focused on her fear that people might hurt her if she could not control their communications with her. She was able to recognize that by overfeeding Jill she was trying to ward off similar fears of being hurt. Eventually she learned to tolerate her daughter's communications and to respond appropriately. As a result Jill was functioning age-appropriately in both cognitive and emotional spheres at the end of her first year of life.

The therapy enabled Mrs. K to tolerate a new state of development in her infant. While Mrs. K had been quite effective in establishing an early nurturant relationship with Jill, characterized by adequate homeostatic patterns and attachment, her own conflicts and marital problems made it hard for her to facilitate her daughter's individuation. However, the marriage and therefore family leadership remain a potential source of further risks for problems in this family unless that situation improves, beginning with the father's achieving abstinence from alcohol.

REFERENCES

Ainsworth, M.D., & Bell, S.M. (1969). Some contemporary patterns of mother-infant interaction in the feeding situation. In A. Abrose (Ed.), *Stimulation in early infancy* (pp. 133–170). New York: Academic Press.

Ainsworth, M.D., Blehar, M., et al. (1968). *Patterns of attachment.* Hillsdale, NJ: Erlbaum.

Bellinger, D., Leviton, A., Waternaux, C., et al. (1987). Longitudinal analysis of prenatal and postnatal lead exposure and early cognitive development. *New England Journal of Medicine, 316,* 1037-1043.

Bowlby, J. (1968-1980). *Attachment and loss.* (Vols. 1, 2 & 3). New York: Basic Books.

Brazelton, T.B. (1973). *Neonatal assessment scale.* London: Spastics Medical Publications.

Brody, E.B. (1981). Can mother-infant interaction produce vulnerability to schizophrenia? *Journal of Nervous and Mental Disease, 169,* 72-81.

Campbell, I.A., Breibmayer, B., & Ranny, C.T. (1986). Disadvantaged single teenage mothers and their children: Consequences of free educational day care. *Family Relations, 35,* 63-68.

Charlesworth, W.R. (1969). The role of surprise in cognitive development. In D. Eckind & J. Flavell (Eds.), *Studies in cognitive development.* Oxford: Oxford University Press.

Cohn, J., & Tronick, E. (1982). Communicative rules and the sequential structure of infant behavior during normal and depressed interaction. In E. Tronick (Ed.), *The development of human communication and the joint regulation of behavior.* Baltimore: Parker Press.

DeCasper, A., & Fifer, W. (1980). Of human bonding: Newborns prefer their mother's voices. *Science, 208,* 1174-1176.

Emde, R., Gaensbauer, T., & Harmon, B. (1976). *Emotional expression in infancy: A behavioral study.* Psychological issues, Monograph series, Vol. X, Monograph No. 37. New York: International Universities Press.

Escalona, S.K., & Leitch, M. (1952). *Early phases of personality development: A nonnormative study of infant behavior.* Washington, DC: Society for Research in Child Development.

Fraiberg, S. (1974). Blind infants and their mothers. An examination of the sign system. In M. Lewis & L. Rosenblum (Eds.), *The effect of the infant on the caregiver.* New York: Wiley.

Fraiberg, S. (1981). *Infant mental health.* New York: Basic Books.

Freud, A. (1966). *Normality and Pathology in Childhood. Assessments of development.* New York: International Universities Press.

Gaensbauer, I., & Sands, S. (1979). Distorted affective communication in abused/neglected infants and their potential impact on caretakers. *Journal of the American Academy of Child Psychiatry, 18,* 236-250.

Goldberg, S., Brachfeld, S., & DiVitto, B. (1979). Feeding, fussing and play: Parent-infant interaction in the first year as a function of newborn medical status. In T. Field, S. Goldberg, D. Stern & A. Sostek (Eds.), *Interactions of high risk infants and children.* New York: Academic Press.

Greenspan, S. (1981). *Psychopathology and adaptation in infancy and early childhood: Principles of diagnosis and preventive intervention.* (Clinical Infant Reports, No. 1). New York: International Universities Press.

Greenspan, S.I., & Pollock, G.H. (Eds.) (1980). *The course of life: Infancy and early childhood.* NIMH. DHHS Publ. No. (ADM) 80-786. Washington, DC: Government Printing Office.

Greenspan, S., & Porges, S. (1984). Psychopathology in infancy and early childhood: Clinical perspectives on the organization of sensory and affective thematic experience. *Child Development, 55,* 49–70.

Izard, C., Kagagan, J., & Zajon, C.R. (1984). *Emotions, cognition and behavior.* New York: Cambridge University Press.

Klaus, M.H., Jerauld, R., Kreger, M.C., et al. (1972). Maternal attachment; importance of the first postpartum days. *New England Journal of Medicine, 286,* 460–463.

Lamb, M. (1978). Influence of the child's mental quality on family interaction during prenatal, perinatal and infancy periods. In R. Lerner & G. Spanier (Eds.), *Child influences on marital and family interaction.* New York: Academic Press.

Lloyd, W. (1950). Group work with mothers in a child development center. *Mental Hygiene, 34,* 620–640.

Meltzoft, A., & Moore, K. (1977). Imitation of facial and manual gestures by human neonates. *Science, 198,* 75–78.

Mendell, D. (1982). *Early female development.* New York: Spectrum Press.

Murphy, L.B., & Moriarty, A.E. (1976). *Vulnerability, coping and growth.* New Haven: Yale University Press.

Pringle, M.K. (1974). Born illegitimate—born at risk. *Journal of Psychosomatic Research, 18,* 229–231.

Sander, L.W. (1962). Issues in early mother-child interaction. *Journal of the American Academy of Child Psychiatry, 1,* 141–166.

Spitz, R. (1957). *No and yes: On the genesis of human communication.* New York: International Universities Press.

Stern, D.N. (1974). The goal and structure of mother-infant play. *Journal of the American Academy of Child Psychiatry, 13,* 402–421.

Stern, D.N. (1985). *The interpersonal world of the infant. A view from psychoanalysis and developmental psychology.* New York: Basic Books.

Thomas, A., & Chess, S. (1977). *Temperament and development.* New York: Brunner/Mazel.

Tronick, E., Als, H., Adamson, L., et al. (1978). The infant's response to entrapment between contradictatory messages in face-to-face interaction. *Journal of the American Academy of Child Psychiatry, 17,*1–13.

5

THE TODDLER FAMILY

BEHAVIORAL ORGANIZATION, INITIATIVE, AND INTERNALIZATION (9-24 MONTHS)

Dennis began to walk and show assertiveness and initiative at the beginning of his second year. At first Ms. M took pride in his accomplishments, but slowly her initial admiration began to give way to envying his "independence."

The visiting nurse had noticed that Ms. M began to overcontrol and criticize Dennis. Her attitude toward her son had shifted from admiration to a fear of his interference with her life, and she felt compelled to curb his initiative. Even more disruptive than this, she had begun to pull away from him emotionally. Dennis gradually changed from an expressive, assertive, satisfied youngster who enjoyed his new motor abilities and his capacity to explore his house to a sober-looking, withdrawn, almost depressed youngster. He was lethargic and showed little curiosity or interest in the world around him. His relationship with his mother became more clinging and dependent, and his sense of autonomy and satisfaction decreased. Ms. M talked about Dennis in terms more appropriate to her relationship with her boyfriend, the father of her son. She was angry that her boyfriend had more freedom in the relationship than she did, and that she had responsibilities that he did not have. She also began to express envious feelings toward the social worker to whom she had been referred because of conflicts with Dennis' father, saying that the worker wore nicer clothes than she had.

Ms. M was a rather attractive, socially sophisticated woman who could converse easily on a variety of subjects. She gave an

overall appearance of assertiveness and competence. She
tended, however, to be suspicious and distrustful, and she
struggled with underlying feelings of envy. Occasionally she
lashed out violently at her boyfriend.

Dennis was constitutionally sound, but seemed irritable.
Earlier Ms. M had cared for his physical needs adequately
and had engaged him in a loving relationship. While she
appeared envious of him, she nonetheless appreciated his
"manly traits," which were similar to certain traits of her
boyfriend; she seemed to enjoy talking about how "assertive
and manly" he could be.

As the infant becomes able to differentiate means from ends,
aspects of self from nonself, and distinguish among significant
others, a capacity for enhanced learning develops, as evidenced
perhaps most strikingly by increased, highly organized imitative
behavior. It is as though the infant/toddler is now "internalizing"
experiences and understanding the immediate surroundings, showing needs, wishes, love and anger, intent and fear. Emotional
systems such as enjoyment or wariness become organized, and
curiosity and exploration are pursued. By 18 months, toddlers
have integrated affective themes such as aggression, love and "taking care" into thier play.

Toddlers are beginning to put "pieces"—abstract emotional cues—
together and realize that they now have an effect on how others
feel. The toddler's ability to take initiative is enriched and facilitated by more imitative behavior and exploratory excursions away
from the secure base of the parents. The capacity for original or
new behavior is enhanced by combining known behaviors or games
with a new one—"going one step beyond the familiar." Trial-and-
error explorations, increased memory, and an appropriate blend
of admiration and limit setting on the parents' part promote the
gradual shift from imitation to identification. The toddler becomes
a more organized, initiating human being; for example, the child
will now actually pull a parent somewhere to show him or her
something. There is also evidence for a beginning psychological
sense of self.

At this stage, the toddler is able to enter into complex interpersonal communications and can share with parents a complicated exploratory game in which the toddler tells the parent to "chase me around the room." The toddler then ducks into another room, then into a closet, and later doubles back to sneak up on the parent, laughing joyfully and jumping into the parent's arms with a hug and a kiss. Obviously, this activity involves exploration, anticipation, pleasure, and so forth. The angry toddler, similarly, can be mischievous in a complex, organized manner, leaving toys scattered around and pretending to be upset when somebody stumbles over them. Also, around 16 to 20 months many toddlers begin to explore their bodies—including genital areas—in a purposeful, deliberate manner, in contrast to the reflexlike mouthing and sucking of the young infant.

Toddlers begin to modulate polarities of feeling and are limited neither to compliant, unassertive, seemingly passive states nor to states of chronic anger or irritability such as biting, poking, kicking things over. Rather, they are able to organize both these polarities in a range of complex behaviors, and respond to the environmental regulation or limit setting. Finally, the growing toddler uses looks, vocalizations, and other affective signals that permit distancing from mother and exploration of surroundings without giving up the security of affective contact with the adult. The practicing of such distancing with the constant availability of the parent's physical closeness provides a transition to the level of development at which the important parent-child affective relationship can be conserved over space and time as part of an organized mental representation, and as such promotes a sense of self and separateness. The toddler can now preserve a mental image of parents, even when they are physically absent.

The facilitating environment at this stage of development admires the toddler's new abilities, greater initiative, and greater originality, and is available, tolerant, and firm when necessary. It follows the youngster's lead, supporting initiatives, and helps to organize one step further than the child can manage on his or her own. The optimal parent not only enters into a game with the happy, smiling toddler but permits game shifts, helping with reorganization if it becomes necessary. Parent and child, for example, may begin looking at pictures together. The toddler then initiates a game in which he or she runs around the room. As the youngster becomes somewhat disorganized, the parent will bring the child back to the point from which they started—looking at pictures and helping the child name objects.

The well-functioning family is not threatened by the child's range of affective expression, but rather helps the youngster integrate affective polarities into meaningful, organized interpersonal responses. When parents see that the youngster maintains an organized noncompliant or chronically aggressive pattern, they will try to identify those events or experiences that may be heightening the child's sense of frustration. Parents may notice that their own work-related stresses have made them emotionally unavailable to the child. This awareness can then allow the parents to respond to the child's negativism and chronic aggression with efforts to shift the youngster's attention to more pleasurable activities rather than dealing with the behavior by scolding or punishing the child. Youngsters' realization that they can escape an unpleasurable state and reenter a more emotionally satisfying relationship with parents helps tie together angry feelings with satisfying experiences —an important step toward separation mastery.

Parents often worry that a child's angry outbursts may be reinforced if they are followed by enjoyable experiences. Limit setting is important during this stage of development when youngsters are experimenting with aggressive, possibly dangerous, behaviors. In particular, if no reason for a youngster's upset state can be discerned, firm limits are necessary to get the child settled down before it may be possible for the youngster to explain his or her outburst. In dealing with aggressive behavior, the key issue is parental involvement and engagement with the child rather than withdrawal, embarrassment or retaliation. The availability of the other parent is important when the child and one parent reach an impasse.

Risks

Problems at this stage may compromise the beginning of internal "psychological" life. Behavior may remain fragmented, related to somatic or external cues, or stereotyped, with the child not developing originality. Intentionality and a sense of self may be stunted. Attention may be unfocused and distractability high, or the child may exhibit chronic temper tantrums, lack of any self-control, poor motor or sensorimotor coordination, chronic negativism, delayed language development, and relationships characterized by aggressive behavior and/or fragmentation and disorganization.

A less severe problem at this stage is that of a child who can organize and experience a very limited range of affects and behaviors with only a rudimentary level of internal imagery. Such children remain tied to concrete, immediate states of need fulfillment and often show rigid and narrow behavior patterns reflecting affective and behavioral polarities such as passive-compliant or aggressive-negativistic. The risk then is failure to develop the intermediary warning and delaying capacities necessary for satisfaction and planning. Sleep disturbances, withdrawal and overcompliance are risk conditions for future trouble.

In the risk-prone environment, the parents may be disorganized or conflicted about the toddler's new independence and originality, or else embarrassed by or ashamed of the child's initiative. There may be only relatively brief casual exchanges: a smile in response to the toddler's smile. But when the toddler tries to develop the reciprocal smiling into a more complex pleasurable game by showing some toys or by asserting him- or herself in some way, there is no response because of the mother's distraction, preoccupation or basic personality limitations. Thus, the toddler's desire to develop and consolidate more organized interaction patterns never receives responsive reinforcement or does so only inconsistently.

Some overprotective mothers may attempt to control the child lest the child control them. Instead of permitting initiative and autonomy, such behaviors are discouraged. Some youngsters then become apathetic and passive; others try to retain the initiative through negative and aggressive behaviors. Still others surrender their interest in the human, animate world for relationships with the more easily controllable inanimate world.

Unacknowledged parental fears of the toddler's increased independence may interfere with development at this stage of childhood.

Commonly such a parent feels abandoned and deprived of the infant's physical closeness. The toddler's new sense of initiative may be misperceived as willfulness, outweighing parental admiration for and pride in the toddler's new abilities. This risk can set the stage for a power struggle for many years to come.

Another danger can develop if parents' conflicts lead them to react adversely to the child's interest in his or her or other people's bodies—what might be viewed as the beginnings of interest in sex. Between 15 and 20 months, children often begin to show interest in the differences between males and females. Scolding or being secretive about bathroom matters can be very upsetting to toddlers, who have a need to explore everything.

Parents who have conflicts about setting limits may create risk conditions. Some, feeling that they have to "tame" their children, undermine initiative and curiosity and, eventually, children's ability to set limits for themselves by overcontrolling them. Other parents, however, have the opposite problem and set no limits at all, relinquishing control. Lastly, parental envy of, or competitiveness with, the fun-loving, carefree toddler can result in overcontrol and stifling of the youngster's initiative.

Preventive Interventions

Intervention at this stage seeks primarily to encourage organization and integration in order to get personality development on an optimal course. It is important to understand those limitations of the youngster and/or the environment that prevent progression toward more complex, organized and integrated ways. Toddlers need to integrate complicated sensory and motor schemes and modulate the intensity of their feelings. They need more than one-person relationships, recognizing mother and father or others as different individuals rather than simply as replacements of one for another, thereby consolidating a sense of self.

It is essential, then, first to uncover possible preexisting difficulties from an earlier stage of development. The intervention plan must then be based on strengthening capacities that have developed inadequately. Whether these are capacities for homeostasis, attachment or differentiation, interventions should be geared to the current level of maturation of the central nervous system and the child's current level of cognitive development. If a youngster can, for example, play in a complex, organized way with a puzzle but is unable to interact warmly and responsively with another person, intervention should not merely involve holding and cuddling or infantile games that would have been appropriate at 7 or 8 months. Rather, one should engage the child's more complexly organized cognitive capacities and emotions to interchanges that label feelings—whether of a doll or the child—thereby helping him or her to express feelings verbally.

In looking at a picture book, for example, mother and child can silently look at pictures with mother turning the pages. All that is required from the toddler is to look. But mother could also combine the child's visual stimulation with verbal description of the pictures. She could further increase the range of stimulation by periodically looking at the youngster and explaining the content of the picture. Toddlers' sensory capacities are far greater than their language competence at this point, and the eager youngster would look from picture to mother and back again, hanging on her every word. At the same time, mother can have the youngster turn the pages, thus enhancing the child's fine motor coordination and enjoying a new accomplishment. As part of this exercise, parents may also be encouraged to have the youngster point out and name the different parts of the picture after the parent does, thus monitoring imitative activity, perceptual-motor coordination, and linguistic development.

Parents can be taught to follow the youngster's lead at times while waiting for opportunities for new affect and behaviors to appear, and at times to create occasions for their natural emergence. A mother who tends to intrude on the child's attempts at mastering new tasks and leaves little opportunity for the spontaneous pleasure of discovery may need help to allow the child to explore on his or her own. The discovery of the inner workings of a toy or of the warm and pleasurable feeling of small fingers in mother's mouth may lead the child to the sought-after spontaneous smile.

Parents may have to experiment to create opportunities for the expression of new emotion. Thus, as parent and child explore a new toy, the parent might demonstrate how the toy can be manipulated. A parent who always sits in a chair might get down on the floor to play with the youngster. Once the youngster shows the first spark of enthusiasm, the parent should be encouraged to show admiration for the new pleasure.

When a toddler has a cautious style and seems to wait for the parent to come to him or her, the parent can learn to wait for the youngster to take the initiative and try to create opportunities for the child to invent some action or game. Another way to encourage greater behavioral organization and initiative is to teach and demonstrate how mother and child can keep in touch with each other even though they are apart. While the youngster explores a room, a prideful glance from mother will often result in a reciprocal show of pleasure by the child; vocalization as signals (prior to clear words) can keep the toddler and caretaker in affective contact despite spatial distance.

When the 14- and 15-month-old youngster is displaying impulsive behavior such as biting, scratching or negativism or showing little initiative and originality, intervention is needed to provide the youngster with an opportunity for alternative behaviors, thus striking a balance between encouraging the child to take the initiative and the setting of limits. Inappropriate parental limitations can be overcome in different ways. An educative approach may help some parents gain an awareness of the youngster's needs that will allow parents to respond in more appropriate ways. If parental character limitations make certain types of affects frightening, or if affects in general are frightening, psychotherapy may be necessary. Gaining awareness that the same emotions parents find frightening in the therapeutic relationship or in life are those they find frightening in their child can increase their tolerance for affects. A focused, time-limited therapeutic effort may be quite effective. Parents' motivation to facilitate their toddler's development, along with a helper's clarification and support, may allow them to tolerate affects in the toddler which may remain frightening to them in other contexts.

Where it is not possible to work with the mother, working with other family members who have a greater range of available affects and a greater tolerance for the youngster's emerging capacities may be appropriate. Just as in the other phases of development, attention must be given to the family's basic needs and to the family as a unit. Problems with housing, finances or health may all play a crucial role in undermining the child's emerging capacities.

The case vignette illustrated a way in which a cognitively competent mother without basic personality disturbance inhibited her child's development by failing to recognize the way in which her own negative feelings had come to dominate their relationship. Indeed, Ms. M's problems with her son may have been a direct consequence of his newly emerging capacities. Unwilling to acknowledge her own envious feelings toward him, and her envious feelings toward the helper, she chose to avoid both relationships, possibly to her own detriment and certainly to her son's disadvantage. Thus the preventive effort failed as she refused further treatment with the social worker or treatment with a male worker toward whom she might have felt less envious.

Family competence was compromised by defective leadership due to the mother's personal problems and the father's apparent refusal to make a formal commitment to mother and son or to participate in the preventive efforts. He would not involve himself in the therapist's efforts to support and repair the family deficiencies. Emotional involvement with the child was disturbed, and the family boundaries remained unclear. Preventive work here would have to include definition of the family structure, working to redirect the mother's efforts to control Dennis into growth-promoting channels, and to help her to accept her parental tasks with or without spousal support. Also, if financial support from her boyfriend were to decline further, adequate provisions for her household and everyday needs from a social agency might be required, which, paradoxically, might afford another opportunity for preventive work. For example, if she were to remain a single parent, a work program for her might entail placing Dennis into a nursery school or daycare, where his development might be furthered rather than hindered. Ms. M, in turn, might derive satisfaction

from a job or training program, obviating her envy of Dennis'
progression and pleasure.

REFERENCES

Bell, S.M. (1970). The development of the concept of the object as related to
    infant-mother attachment. *Child Development, 41,* 291–311.
Bowen, M. (1974). Toward the differentiation of self in one's family of origin. In
    F. Andes & J. Lorio (Eds.), *Georgetown family symposium papers* (Vol. 1). Washington,
    DC: Georgetown University Press.
Greenspan, S., Weider, S., Lieberman, A., et al. (1986). *Infants in multi-risk families:
    Case studies of preventive intervention.* Clinical Infant Reports, No. 3. New York:
    International Universities Press.
Huntington, D. (1982). *Developmental review.* The EPDST Program, US Department
    of Health, Education, and Welfare. Washington, DC: US Government Print-
    ing Office.
Kagan, J. (1981). *The second year.* Cambridge, MA: Harvard University Press.
Mahler, M. (1972). On the first three phases of the separation-individuation
    process. *International Journal of Psychoanalysis, 53,* 333–338.
Matas, L., Arend, R., & Stroufe, L.A. (1978). Continuity of adaptation in the second
    year: The relationship between quality of attachment and later competent
    functioning. *Child Development, 49,* 547–556.
Provence, S. (Ed.) (1983). *Infants and parents: Case studies.* Clinical Infant Reports
    No. 2. New York: International Universities Press.
Rosenblum, L. (Ed.) (1974). *The origins of fear.* New York: Wiley.
Werner, H., & Kaplan, B. (1963). *Symbol formation.* New York: Wiley.
Winnicott, D.W. (1953). Transitional objects and transitional phenomena. In
    Collected papers: Through pediatrics to psychoanalysis. New York: Basic Books,
    1960.
Zahn-Waxler, C., Radke-Yarrow, M., & King, R.A. (1979). Child rearing and children's
    prosocial initiations towards victims of distress. *Child Development, 50,* 319–330.

6

THE PRESCHOOL FAMILY

REPRESENTATION, ELABORATION AND SYMBOLIZATION OF RELATIONSHIPS (20-48 MONTHS)

Jennifer, 20 months old, was able to string together a number of words and occasionally use a personal pronoun. She was attempting to engage in symbolic play. She would bring dolls to her mother and attempt to develop some interaction between one doll and another, asking mother to hold one doll while she held the other. Or she would bring a toy telephone and say "hello" and "good-bye," wanting her mother to play a reciprocal role. However, whenever Jennifer attempted to play these games with mother, Mrs. N rather abruptly shifted gears and suggested that perhaps her daughter was "hungry or tired and needed to sleep." She tended to respond to her daughter's symbolic communications by bringing them down to a concrete level, at which she was obviously more comfortable. Jennifer, in response to this, became negative and aggressive, started to kick and bite and to give up her symbolic activity, used fewer words, played with blocks more than with dolls, and in general imitated the mother's concrete style.

Mrs. N was a rather assertive, warmly engaging mother with limited intellectual capacity who tended to relate to her own emotional needs in a very concrete fashion. Although she tended to use denial and avoidance around emotional conflict, she was able to maintain a reasonable relationship with her husband whose personality was organized along similar lines. When Jennifer was born, Mrs. N was very excited and, in an obsessive way, wanted to make sure that Jennifer would have just the right food, temperature in the house, clothing, and so on. Mrs. N seemed to be very concerned with providing appropriate physical care because an older daughter had learning and behavioral problems at school and Mrs. N felt that she could guarantee a better adjustment for Jennifer by making sure that she fed and clothed her properly. Whenever Mrs. N discussed her feelings, she would quickly bring the discussion around to such concrete needs as food and appropriate medication. In spite of these limitations, she had achieved a rich emotional involvement with her infant and derived satisfaction from it.

The visiting nurse recognized the overclose relationship between Jennifer and her controlling mother. The nurse noted that the mother failed to support Jennifer's emerging symbolic activities and felt that the child needed nursery school experience. The mother declined this recommendation—"Jennifer isn't ready for that." The nurse alerted the pediatrician to the problem, who, in turn, wanted a developmental assessment.

Adaptive Tasks

With the achievement of representational capacity at around 18–30 months, an ability to conserve internal representations of animate and inanimate objects emerges; an increased behavioral, emotional, cognitive, and interpersonal repertoire is developing. Personal pronouns and the ability to say "no" appear. The child can now organize mental images to search for inanimate and animate objects and can recall events as well as emotional experiences. Exclusive need-fulfilling behavior recedes, and cooperation with, and concern for, others begins to show. The adaptive child now has an ability to form and arrange mental representations into organized units of increasing range and depth. For this child, "out of sight" no longer means "out of mind." Experience becomes the basis whereby one segment of reality or fantasy can be integrated with another, and the mental manipulation of symbols gradually emerges.

Such experiences can be observed at the earliest stage of representational capacity. For example, the degree to which not only pleasurable experience but also assertive and exploratory experience are represented at a symbolic level can be noted as a toddler is able to look for something hidden in a drawer or can ask for a favorite cookie, pointing to the jar. The degree to which angry protest and negative behavior become organized at a symbolic level can also be observed as growing toddlers not only use "no" more frequently, but begin to show a selective capacity to "know" what they want; they can say "no" to eating chicken and "yes" to ice cream and candy. It is unusual for toddlers just past the second birthday to use complex sentences, but the juxtaposition of "no" with the demand for something is quite clear.

As youngsters begin to use words, experiences are described in most basic terms: "doll" or "cake." A few months later modifying words may have been mastered—the toddler saying "eat cake, happy" as he or she holds a pretend tea party. Before long the toddler may communicate in a full sentence. Thus, with the child's growing vocabulary, more and more experiences can be described.

The child will begin to express personal interactions as well. The toddler might embellish "this is a doll" with "she is smiling because the mommy doll is holding her," and then ask, "Pick me up. Hold me." The toddler who begins to use personal pronouns and verbs in an action-oriented sense—"I want you to do . . ." "Please get me . . ."—uses language instrumentally, and, in a broader sense, translates symbolic capacities into interactions. On a nonverbal level, the toddler who plays a trick on mother—hiding her pocketbook when she is about to go shopping and then laughing as mother looks confused—obviously has an excellent capacity for symbolic elaboration of interactions involving planning and anticipation, even though not a single word may be uttered. The use of words is not the only indication of symbolic activity. Play and interactions which involve complex planning and obvious manipulation of "thoughts" are other ways through which the child shows the existence of this mental capacity, leading toward the emergence of a "person."

Parents should now converse with the child without the use of baby talk. The interactional dramas that are elaborated, whether in reality or play, encompass multiple themes involving various behavioral and affective domains. There is a great deal of difference between the youngster who can interact symbolically only in aggressive ways and the youngster who shows symbolic activity across all the age-expected range of thematic and affection communication; examples include dolls fighting and a doctor fixing a hurt doll.

Determining whether the youngster is using an adaptive capacity appropriately is important. Can the child manipulate symbols in order to make needs known? Can he or she communicate appropriately with parents and peers and tolerate more frustration than at earlier stages? Do these new capacities help him or her to become more explorative and independent and to master new situations, or do they serve only to make the youngster more skillful in a negative way? Generally, if the child can show symbolically the range of human experience in an age-appropriate balance— reflecting life's polarities of love and hate, passivity and activity, etc.—such a child is coping in a constructive way. If the symbolic range is loaded toward one end of the experiential world—toward negativistic and angry experiences only, or superficially pleasurable, passive, compliant experiences—there may be maladaptive trends developing. Similarly, if symbols are used predominantly in relation to the inanimate world, and in turn the child turns away from people, a risk for maladaption exists.

These crucial developments can be observed in the relationship with the parents and with other adults such as a daycare person or a relative. More complex interactions should also be seen with siblings, and will gradually emerge in peer relationships. For example, 2-year-olds can play together and begin sharing. A dialogue between two children as they negotiate who is going to have control over a toy will often break down, and they will get angry and fight and cry. In the process, however, there are islands of ideational activity that make their lives more sophisticated in all spheres.

Family and Environment

At this stage, the growth-promoting environment reads, responds to, and encourages symbolic elaboration across a range of behavioral and emotional communications and is, at the same time, available for age-expected dependency needs and regressions. The goal is to facilitate representational or symbolic modes in deep, stable and individually unique configurations and, thus, to help the child become a person.

Parents should engage the youngster through language, encouraging descriptive words and helping identify the inanimate and animate worlds, for example, "That's a car," "That's Mommy." Parents who engage their child on the symbolic level will respond, "Yes, that is Bill," and will try to take the conversation a step further by saying, "There is Joan. What do you want to say to her?" The use of language to represent personal interactions is encouraged. When the youngster says, "Please pick me up, Mommy," the parent will respond, "Yes, I'll come and pick you up" or "Sorry, I can't pick you up now. I'm cooking, but I'll pick you up in a minute."

As already mentioned, the use of symbols is not only verbal but can also be encouraged in play activities as children begin to show through their play the ability to develop themes or dramas that symbolically express their ideas, feelings, wishes. The 25-month-old toddler may hug a doll and say that the doll is Mommy or that he or she is Mommy holding baby sister. When a little older, the child may have a tea party with all the dolls involved in a complex drama the youngster has devised. Parents can enter into these games and help to make them more complex. Father may sit down and participate in the tea party, and when the child asks, "Do you want some more tea?" Father can respond with gestures or words or both, "Of course I want more tea; it is very good." He then takes the cup to his mouth and pretends to drink. By his warmth and interest, he is encouraging the use of this symbolic involvement. When, in contrast, the bored father withdraws behind his newspaper, the child may throw the tea set to the floor and begin grabbing at father's knee or trying to crawl up into his lap, giving up the symbolic mode for the concrete.

Once representational capacity has been established, supporting its elaboration across a range of animate and inanimate experience is in order. With respect to the inanimate world, the parent can supply the youngster with a puzzle that can be described, manipulated, and creatively transformed. Such play things should have qualities that appeal to the child's various senses. Textured, brightly colored toys will engage the child's sense of touch and vision and encourage description and labeling.

In the animate world, elaboration of representational modes around pleasure, assertiveness, curiosity, protest and the like need to be encouraged. If the parent shows little or no interest in the youngster's assertiveness and curiosity, the child may gradually conclude that exploration does not elicit human interaction. The parent who responds to the aggressive, demanding or angry youngster by dealing with him or her concretely by physical means or, worse, figuratively abandoning the youngster by refusing to interact or talk will discourage a child's use of representational capacity with respect to these affects. This is not to suggest that limit setting is not vital, because limit setting with "meaning" enhances the youngster's symbolic capacity and boundary awareness.

Parents further need to respect the child's emerging capacities to delay gratification. Along with providing a basic sense of security, parents must also recognize that the child's newly emerging capacity for delay will not develop if needs are immediately satisfied in a concrete fashion. A balance between the provision of support, postponement and limit setting is important. The frustrated youngster's temper tantrums and other disorganized expressions of anger need to be accepted up to a point, so that these feelings and experiences can be elaborated on a representational level. However, firm limit setting—including, at times, suitable punishment—is also necessary if the child is to modulate intense feelings and learn what others will and will not tolerate and learn the rudiments of rules. The spoiled youngster who is given everything and whose temper tantrums go unchallenged may find little motivation for dealing with the world at higher levels of representation, and will fail to modulate intense feelings, let alone appreciate the needs of others.

Risks

Children at risk for maldevelopment at this stage exhibit a relative inability to form mental representations. Their imagery will not coalesce into organized experiential units, and language capacity remains at the descriptive or concrete level. They have difficulty expressing inner thoughts and feelings or complex interactions. Symptoms to watch for include: 1) disorganized emotional and motor responses; 2) chronic, unrelenting clinging with suspension of exploratory behavior; 3) primitive aggressive behavior such as biting or scratching; 4) fearfulness; and 5) either interpersonal clinging or withdrawal. Such disorders in the early organization of internal mental representations can profoundly impair basic ego functions, as seen later on in adult psychotic and borderline patients.

At an extreme level, severely regressive behavior may surface, or the effort to relate to others is given up and autistic-like behavior may appear. Sensorimotor integration, affective reactions and previously acquired interpersonal skills can all become fragmented if maladaptation in this phase disrupts development.

The youngster whose cognitive development has reached a level of verbal imitation, but who lacks the capacity to represent human interactional experience mentally, may speak either nonsense syllables or recognizable words that bear little relationship to one another. Instead of saying, "Come here, candy," the disturbed child may say "eat" as a signal of hunger followed by "dog" or "horse" and point to toys around the room. This suggests that the most rudimentary form of purposefulness at a representational level has not been mastered.

At a less severe level, some youngsters may attain representational capacity but have limitations in another area. Some may be able to represent the inanimate world. They can describe inanimate objects, talk in sentences, and recall a game seen the day before. These same children, however, may be withdrawn from the animate world and uninvolved in human relationships or, when involved, may behave more like 1-year-olds, unable to demonstrate the organized interpersonal behavior expected at 20 months and beyond. Not infrequently, youngsters can do complicated puzzles and use words in short sentences, but shy away from any relationship to parents or siblings, preferring to play by themselves. In a play group such a child may go off and withdraw in a corner. When coaxed into interpersonal activity, he or she becomes aggressive toward the other children, biting or throwing toys, crawling and uttering nonsense sounds instead of using age-appropriate language.

At a somewhat higher level, youngsters may have developed a representational capacity in both the inanimate and animate spheres but show limitations in certain areas of human experience. They may use symbolic modes only around negativism, dominance and aggression, always saying "no" or "I want that." This children seem always to look solemn, stubborn and angry and show little range of pleasure. Their relationships with their parents or siblings are characterized by demands and temper tantrums. Other youngsters on the same level use symbolic modes only in a passive, compliant, and superficially pleasurable way. They may be overly dependent, wanting to sit in a parent's lap. They may lack exploratory capacity and an ability to be firm or assertive. It is rare for them to be negativistic, angry or to say "no" adamantly. They have not mastered age-typical separations.

Others may oscillate between compliant states of superficial pleasure and temper tantrums. They show little ability to moderate either of these extremes or to bring both sides of their nature to a consecutive set of experiences. They do not exhibit hearty laughter and joyous compliance at one point during a game with a loved parent and assertive demandingness shortly thereafter.

Some children show severe limitations in exploration, a trait or fear usually combined with excessive dependency needs. For example, a youngster may play a complicated game with dolls as long as he or she is sitting in mother's lap. When separated from the mother even briefly, this child will take to crawling or playing nonsymbolic games such as aimlessly rolling a ball or throwing toys on the floor. He or she may walk around without purpose or look for infantile interactions which do not require symbolic activity.

In contrast to the growth-promoting environment, the deficient environment fails to support the development of representational capacities, or at least the full range of age-appropriate, experience-promoting, deep, stable, and individualistic patterns. At its most extreme, there may be complete failure to engage the youngster representationally, either at the descriptive or the interactional level. There is no encouragement to use words to describe objects or people, and probably no reading to and with the child. The youngster's imitation of words and attempts to use other symbols are not reinforced or are undermined in such a deficient environment. As the child begins to attach words to objects, the parents become preoccupied or withdrawn. Oblivious to their child's needs, the parent(s) give(s) little or no feedback or support. On the other hand, parents may overcontrol a child, teaching or intruding excessively. They may insist that the child name everything in sight. In such instances, the bewildered toddler is likely to withdraw into a negativistic stance, refusing to participate even at the descriptive level.

More common are parents who do not encourage the representation of personal interactions. If they are willing to engage the youngster at all, it is around concrete activities such as holding or feeding. When the child says, "I want dinner now," rather than responding, "Not yet, you have to wait a little," the parent may ignore the youngster's verbal communication altogether, leaving the frustrated youngster to feel that there is no choice but to resort to earlier behaviors such as crying or angry tantrums, typical of a 3- or 4-month-old infant when hungry. If the parent does respond to the child's symbolic communication of hunger, it may be in an overly punitive, intrusive and controlling way—"No, get out of here," accompanied by a slap, so that the youngster finds representational modes of communicating highly unrewarding. In such instances, resorting once again to aggressive or earlier concrete ways of expression may seem to be the only way open to the toddler.

Emerging representational capacity may be undermined by misreading or distorting the symbolic communication of the child. The child may come in smiling, saying "cookie" and open his or her mouth in expectation and point to the cookie jar. Instead of experiencing this as an opportunity for her youngster to elaborate, mother experiences it as an assault on her freedom—"The little monster just wants to get my goat, knowing that I am reading my magazine." Or a parent, uncomfortable with this kind of angry reaction, might simply respond with a non sequitur, "What a nice day it is outside," and a suggestion that the youngster look at the sun. Such lack of responsiveness, or distorted or unrelated responsiveness, may undermine the very foundation of the representational system.

Sometimes, some areas of representational elaboration may be supported while others are undermined. Parents with conflicts over aggression, for example, may be able to support the symbolic elaboration of dependency needs or pleasurable pursuits, whereas aggressive expressions may be met with rejection, withdrawal or punishment.

Preventive Interventions

In the early toddler phase, frontline practitioners and others can look quickly at: 1) the child's readiness to get involved in make-believe play with other people as social partners, and 2) the child's capacity to use language around emotional themes.

Obviously the broad principle is to help the child master the adaptive tasks outlined. There are two simple and very concrete things that can be suggested as a sort of trial balloon and that indicate how flexible a family is and how adaptable the child is. Often when there is a problem—anything from temper tantrums to aggressive behavior, night terrors, refusal to go to sleep, refusal to cooperate in toilet training, or other kinds of common symptomatic behavior—the first thing that is relatively easy to do is to tell the parents to have more "floor time" with the child. Floor time involves pretend-play activity and trying, as much as possible, to elicit words elaborating on the make-believe. The pretend-play should involve interaction, with the parent basically following the child's lead. Such pretend-play sessions have to be set up for at least 20 minutes to a half-hour. It may take a child 15 minutes to get relaxed with the parent; the child may spend the first 15 minutes just knocking blocks down before more complicated play begins. It is better to have half-hour sessions with the parents just sitting and the child doing nothing—the parent may be making a few overtures saying,

"Gee, the blocks look interesting." But the parent should try to follow the child's lead, never taking over, but stimulating—"That's interesting. Wow! What are we going to do next? What's the dolly doing?" The parent should not bombard the child with questions but should provide a sort of empathetic collaboration—"What's going to happen next?" "What's going on here?"

Parental inadequacies may be due to preoccupation with their own work, ignorance of what to do at this developmental stage, conflicts around entering into the representational mode, or severe personality problems. When the problem is a simple lack of know-how, education with follow-up support may suffice. Modeling can be used as an important part of such teaching. Where parental conflicts exist, the didactic how-to approach may need to be combined with an exploration of these conflicts as well. If parental pathology is severe, psychotherapy will be necessary to deal with some of the causes of such difficulties. It is not always necessary for the parents to reach a total resolution of their difficulties before they can alter their behavior to benefit the child. With support and encouragement from child workers, teachers or clinicians, willing parents often borrow the skills of the "other" to use with their children while also engaged in resolving their own basic difficulties.

If there are residual difficulties such as overattachment to parental figures or an inadequate capacity to control the expression of feelings or hyperexcitability or irritability, the principle is the same: assist the child in negotiating these earlier issues while encouraging the development of representational capacities. The youngster who has not achieved internal regulation and is either hyperexcitable or excessively irritable may require a good deal of physical holding even at 20-24 months, but he or she also needs experiences that are consistent with newly emerging representational capacities. A child with shallow attachments, who is only superficially and impersonally involved with another person, may require extra wooing.

If the difficulties are more limited, another pattern of preventive intervention is required. There are youngsters who are developing and elaborating their symbolic and representational capacities yet may lack a sense of exploration or curiosity, or they may be overly passive and compliant, or only aggressive and negativistic. The task, then, is to see which issues interfere with elaboration in the constricted areas and to develop a program to help encourage and support symbolic elaboration in these areas. It may be that the parents are uncomfortable with pleasure and dependency and are strongly focused instead on success and assertion. At times such parents may simply need to be taught how to support development of representational capacity in these underused modes. At other times, however, parental conflicts will have to be dealt with directly before the parents can learn to support the child in certain areas.

Developmental assessment showed that Jennifer was not using symbolic modes, that she was fearful of strangers, and that in doll play fathers or males did not seem to exist for her. The pediatrician then decided to contact Jennifer's father directly. Mr. N was very receptive and eager to help and participate in any program as long as it did not interfere with his work; he could not afford any time off. Mr. N indicated that he felt excluded from the mother-child dyad and would appreciate help in becoming an active parent. It was decided that the office nurse would visit the family, and she succeeded over several visits to wean Jennifer from her mother, and vice versa. Also, by demonstrating "floor time," the nurse introduced Jennifer and her parents to active play and how to respond to the child's wants and ideas. Jennifer thus progressed to the symbolic stage of development.

The marriage needed attention too, and gradually Mrs. N was able to forgo her obsessive mothering, resume more of a spousal role, and permit joint family leadership. Over time the other system areas improved accordingly, communication in particular.

SYMBOLIZATION OF RELATIONSHIPS (30-48 MONTHS)

Cindy, just under 3 years, was a bright, energetic little girl who was waking up with panic-provoking nightmares. She insisted on being comforted by her mother, often for hours, before she would return to sleep. As the nightmares grew in intensity, her mother was required to be with her for increasing lengths of time. Finally her parents sought consultation. History revealed that Cindy had been quite slow in developing sensory, motor and cognitive capacities but had seemed to accelerate between 18 and 24 months. Cognitively she was well ahead of the 3-year-old range, and during the day, at least, was able to deal appropriately with a variety of routine activities.

The family physician learned that when Cindy was about 22 months old, her mother, who had been working part-time, rather suddenly decided to return to work full-time. At the same time her father was coming home progressively later, at 8:00 or 9:00 in the evening. The nightmares had begun shortly after the mother's resumption of full-time work. Mrs. L felt that she had given up her career long enough and now needed to return to it before it was too late. She was a highly competent, assertive, matter-of-fact woman who seemed unable to relax and was uncomfortable about showing the more dependent, passive and intimate aspects of her personality. Mr. L was similar. He was a very obsessive man, and very invested in his daughter's cognitive development. He angrily demanded to find out what was wrong. The physician felt that only expert evaluation by a specialist would satisfy these parents and enable them to heed recommendations.

Observing mother and daughter in a joint play session showed mother helping her daughter name objects, thus interacting at a descriptive representational level. But when Cindy tried to interact symbolically around an emotional theme, Mrs. L usually returned to the descriptive symbolic level. Mrs. L was unable to respond to some symbolic themes. When Cindy wanted mother to hold one doll while a second doll fed it, mother could cooperate. But when Cindy tried to play out an aggressive scene and pretended that an animal was after mother's nose, Mrs. L abruptly grabbed the animal and started attacking her daughter. While reluctant to engage in differentiated symbolic activity in general, mother was particularly adverse to aggressive themes. Whenever Cindy turned to aggression, Mrs. L would take charge immediately and put her daughter down and return to a descriptive level. Cindy was tense throughout the session with mother and showed little range of affect. This little girl's symbolic elaboration and differentiation were supported in some emotional areas but compromised rather dramatically in others.

Cindy's history revealed that there were almost no power struggles or displays of stubbornness or negativism on her part during the day. Nor was there much opportunity for this little girl to engage her parents along the more assertive domain because they were out of the house. Thus, the power struggles seemed to occur at night, when she would awaken frightened and demand that mother stay with her, and mother, perplexed, yielded to her daughter's demands.

Adaptive Tasks

One of the adaptive tasks between 30 and 36 months of age is not only the gradual elaboration of the internal world and of emotional ideas but learning to organize these emotional ideas into differentiated categories. A category of emotional ideas develops having to do with the self and all those attendant feelings and tensions, and also a category of emotional ideas concerning relationships with mommy or daddy, little brother Johnny or sister Susie, or little friend Alice. No longer do a lot of floating ideas in the internal world of the child come out only haphazardly; they are now becoming organized into categories which have spatial and temporal features to them as well. The important thing about this beginning organization of categories is that it goes beyond instrumental language, so that the child begins to express ideas and feelings spontaneously. The ability to perceive, label, organize and communicate experience, whether that experience is coming from the outside or from within, sets the basis for fundamental personality functions. These basic personality functions should develop between 30 and 48 months and include testing reality (knowing what is real from make-believe), being able to cooperate in getting dressed and so forth, and listening to instructions. Children who are able to categorize emotional ideas thoroughly enjoy fantasies, even to the point of getting lost in them, but if somebody asks, "Is that real or make-believe?" they can say, "Oh, that's just make-believe." Thus, by 30 months, and sometimes even earlier, children have the ability to shift gears and say, "That's pretend," demonstrating that they can test reality.

The ability to control impulses is based on the capacity to recognize "an acting me," a "me who acts" in the world, with an understanding of what the consequences are: Do this, it will make my little brother cry. This ability to set limits involves categorizing ideas and, as an acting person, considering the consequences they are likely to elicit from the environment. Thus impulse control emerges.

A more stable mood emerges between 30 and 48 months, ideally one of optimism. The 2-year-old has all these little islands of ideas that change rather quickly, so greater mood lability is expectable. As the child gets closer to 3 years old, the islands of emotion are coalescing into the categories described. There is a sense of self that has to do with many islands of feelings, many islands of self-perception and self-ideas, so there is a more stable mood pattern as the child gets closer to 3 and 4 years of age. The sense of property—"what's mine"—is related to this category of understanding that there is "a me" and "a you." Ownership does not have to do just with ideas, but also with things. With the ability to categorize ideas and make things happen, positive self-esteem develops because the child is operating on the world. The child now knows he or she can control parts of that world, not just the world of ideas, but that ideas can be translated into actions, and he or she can make things happen. Concentration becomes more focused, and persistence and ability to plan for the future appear, again related to the ability to categorize things along with the dimension of time. Children close to 3½ or 4 years old can anticipate that if they do something now, it will lead to something else happening in the future—at least the near future.

These adaptive tasks are the foundation stones of basic personality or ego functions and should be learned by the age of 3 or 4. As part of this development, the interest in the body changes from purely behavioral concerns in the toddler stage to an emotional/

ideational interest that is somewhat disorganized around ages 2
to 2½. It becomes more organized with the ability to categorize
ideas and perceive one's own body in its full complexity. There is
great interest in different body parts—particularly the sexual parts
—that begins as early as 8 months of life on an exploratory behavioral level, which now takes on ideational significance in this new
phase of emotional and ideational categorization. This interest in
body parts extends to others—to children of the opposite sex, but
especially to parents.

Risks

The possessiveness toward the mother should recede around the
age of 4 for both boys and girls, although the latter can and likely
will shift their main interest toward the father. Boys can strive to be
like their fathers, but also must accept the mother's primary relationship with the father. The physical closeness to and interaction
with either or both parents should be modulated and become
more verbal and cooperative, like doing things together. If these
relational transitions are not properly negotiated, if one or the
other parent continues with predominantly physical interaction
with the child, he or she may feel sexually stimulated. Then,
incestuous proclivities may persist, a serious risk for psychosexual
maldevelopment. Actual incest between a parent and child or with
an older sibling is evidence of severe family pathology, which must
be remedied, if necessary with the involvement of the legal system.
Preventive efforts then can be directed only toward alleviating the
traumatic consequences for all concerned.
     Another important risk factor at this stage for the child and
family is that the child may continue on a concrete behavior-
discharge level and not move to functional use of language in
emotional realms. Showing a lot of make-believe play without
progressing to the categorization of emotional ideas constitutes a
handicap in basic personality formation. The observer should look
at each of the domains of the child's functioning—with siblings,
peers, family, other adults—in order to see the use of emotional

ideas and their categorization in terms of reality testing and impulse control.

Preventive Interventions

The 30- to 48-month-old is beginning to show signs of differentiating reality from fantasy, and signs of impulse control, of more stable mood, and of positive self-esteem. If none of that is happening, the observer should wonder what is going on in the child or in the family. Some children, because of a neurological problem, may not comprehend very well and may need more practice, but the deficiencies may also reflect family malfunctioning, a disturbed parent, a conflicted marriage, lack of parenting know-how, or any combination of these.

If parents are unresponsive to preventive approaches because of their own earlier experiences and limitations in the flexibility of their personality structures, a combination of educational and therapeutic interventions may be necessary. Work or play therapy with the child may also be indicated if the difficulties in developing a reality orientation, in consolidating representational differentiation, and in separation competence are rooted in earlier development deficits.

In Cindy's family the mother felt unsupported by her spouse, who seemed not much interested in his daughter except for her intellectual development. Leadership was deficient and not conjoint. Mrs. L's earlier closeness to her growing daughter, followed by abrupt separation, interfered with boundary developments. Cindy felt abandoned instead of having her sense of self enhanced and of feeling securely held by the family and its boundaries. The emotional climate was disturbed through the mother's overattachment and sense of guilt as well as by the father's distance. Communication was held on a concrete level, and the tasks of helping Cindy with emotional and cognitive elaboration and expression were not met.

The family physician felt that expert help was needed, and she informed Mr. L directly that without revealing Cindy's identity she had consulted with a well-known family therapist concerning Cindy's problem. The consultant agreed with the physician's assessment. The consultant advised that Cindy might well be headed for serious trouble and would not be ready for kindergarten if family life continued in the present pattern. This dire prognosis had its effect, and Mr. L agreed to meet with the family therapist and to get his wife to go along. After an initial evaluation, Mr. and Mrs. L accepted continued family therapy as well as some play sessions for Cindy. The nightmares subsided gradually, and a year later Cindy's development seemed on an age-appropriate course. Parental leadership had become conjoint, and Cindy's father could tolerate some of her moves to be close to him. The generational boundary had become appropriately permeable, and emotionality and some warmth had begun to grow in the family. There was even some talk about having another child. Communication was now triadic and enjoyable for all. From such a base Cindy should be ready for peer relationships, playground and school.

Because of this physician's knowledge of the family and their prestige orientation, she should overcome parental resistance to, and doubts about, preventive intervention by herself or the staff. Invoking the help of a prestigious expert was the correct prescription for this family, although the preventive treatment could have been carried out by others.

REFERENCES

Darlington, R.B., Royce, J.M., Snipper, A.S., Murray, A.W., & Lazar, J. (1980). Preschool programs and later school competence of children from low income families. *Science, 208,* 202–204.

Erikson, E.H. (1939). Configuration in play—clinical notes. *Psychoanalytic Quarterly, 6,* 139–214.

Fraiberg, S. (1969). Libidinal object constancy and mental representation. *Psychoanalytic Studies of the Child, 24,* 9–47.

Freud, A. (1965). *Normality and pathology in childhood.* New York: International Universities Press.

Gouin-Decarie, T. (1965). *Intelligence and affectivity in early childhood: An experimental study of Jean Piaget's object concept and object relations.* New York: International Universities Press.

Greenspan, S. (1979). *Intelligence and adaptation: An integration of psychoanalytic and Piagetian development psychology.* Psychological Issues Monograph 47/48. New York: International Universities Press.

Hoffman, M.L. (1982). Development of prosocial motivation: Empathy and guilt. In L. Eisenberg (Ed.), *The development of prosocial behavior.* New York: Academic Press.

Ludek, S. (1972). Longitudinal study of Piaget's developmental stages and the concept of regression. II. *Journal of Personality Assessment, 36,* 468–478.

Mahler, M.S. (1972). Rapprochement subphase of the separation-individuation process. *Psychoanalytic Quarterly 41,* 487–506.

Mahler, M., Pine, F., & Bergman, A. (1975). *The psychological birth of the human infant.* New York: Basic Books.

Nicholitch, L. (1981). Towards symbolic functioning. Structure of early pretend-games and potential parallels with language. *Child Development, 52,* 386–388.

Peller, L. (1954). Libidinal phases, ego development and play. *Psychoanalytic Studies of the Child, 9,* 178–198.

Piaget, J., & Inhelder, B. (1969). *The psychology of the child.* New York: Basic Books.

Provence, S. (1980). Direct observation and psychoanalytic developmental psychology: The child from one to three. In S. Greenspan & G. Pollock (Eds.), *The course of life. Vol. I. Infancy and early childhood.* Washington, DC: Government Printing Office.

Vygotsky, L. (1962). *Thought and language.* Boston: M.I.T. Press.

7

FAMILY UNITY—GRADE SCHOOL CHILDREN

The after-school activities coach was the first person to voice concern about 10-year-old Randy. Although Randy's academic work at his private school was consistently good, he was having trouble handling team activities. He called attention to himself by whining, complaining about other children, and always blaming another for his own difficulties. The other boys, in response, began to tease and avoid him. Aware of Randy's distress, the coach tried to reach the parents to discuss his behavior. The coach learned that Randy lived only with his responsible 15-year-old sister. Their divorced mother, a career journalist, lived and worked in a city several hours away Monday through Friday but telephoned home every night. On weekends she cooked meals for the entire week. Her choice of private school for Randy had been made because it offered an intensive after-school program where he would be supervised. She also appreciated the individual attention paid to each child academically. Once reached, mother seemed very surprised to hear of Randy's difficulties.

Behavior in grade school can serve as an index of socioemotional development. Three areas of rapid growth and development for this age group are: 1) central nervous system maturation, 2) emotional growth, and 3) social development and interaction.

Central nervous system maturation includes mastering academic, gross and fine motor skills. Success in reading and basic mathematics provides easily measured indices in the school setting and at home. Motor skills can be roughly estimated at school by observing athletic attempts and manual dexterity.

Emotional growth can also be indexed by specific behaviors. Children at this age learn how to balance continued closeness with their families with branching out into peer friendships. Sufficient separation from the family to permit the child to identify with same-sex children occurs naturally in healthy children from secure families.

The third important development issue is social interaction. The grade school child must adapt to external rules as well as establish internal rules. Participation in team sports, competitions, and secret clubs indicates how a particular child is faring socially. The most obvious indicator in school is the child's classroom behavior and ability to follow rules when playing with peers.

Children who experience a solid relationship with one or more nurturant parents move into the grade school setting with a mixture of anticipation, trust and trepidation. If fostered adequately, trust in adults develops during the early years of life and allows the child to experience teachers as both authority figures and caring helpers. For example, the demands placed on the first grader are often much more difficult than those faced in preschool or kindergarten. As one new first grader said to his 3-year-old sister in day care, "All you gotta do is don't hit anybody and be good. I gotta do that *and* sit at my desk and be quiet and write my letters over and over. It's not fair!"

By the fifth year, the child has a well-established grasp of reality. A 5- or 6-year-old is capable of both being swept away by fantasy and of stepping back to say, "That's not real." At this time, the child's major interests concern important human issues: sex, aggression, power, curiosity, discovery and emerging morality. Triangular patterns of relationships show up again and again in play: feeling left out, wanting to leave someone else out, or fantasies of getting rid of a third person in a triangle. The child's play has rich, complex and integrated stories, for example, games where the child first takes care of a sibling in a loving fashion, then becomes an attacking monster, then becomes concerned with retaliation and protects the sibling again. Parents and teachers can sense a slight shift in 4- to 6-year-old children from interests in physical abilities and the child's own body to how it compares to others' bodies, especially sexual parts and activities, including an intense interest in what goes on "behind closed doors." Fear of body injury takes over, although earlier fears of loss of approval and fears of separation can still trouble the child. A new emerging fear for the 5- and 6-year-old is loss of the sense of self-esteem and dignity, where before there was fear of disapproval. A 5- or 6-year-old can say, "I'm very mad at me." Play is now well organized, rich with symbols, and incorporates major themes and fears.

The inner world of the 7- and 8-year-old is even more organized. Parents and teachers can see a slight shift in emphasis from pleasurable pursuits toward themes of control. A healthy youngster strikes a balance between pleasure and control—a balance that remains rather fluid. A sense of morality—what's right and wrong—is emerging but is still unstable, being usually rather strict, even harsh. These are the children who cannot tolerate a cheater, who are mortified (and therefore heartless) if a classmate has a bathroom "accident," and who may insist there is only *one* way to do something. The emerging morality and the developing sense of need for control cause these children to deny previous interests. Interest in roles—"what I am"—is emerging, as is a secure body image. Some parents are surprised at the sex-stereotyped roles children at this age choose for themselves.

The stories of a 9- and 10-year-old are rich with details, motivation and plot. A 10-year-old may retell the Nancy Drew mystery she read complete with verbatim dialogue and explanations of how the villains chose their victim. Stories of ball games or parties where adult roles are imitated are also presented in a detailed, organized manner. A story is presented with little or no fragmentation, and for the first time the adult can hear the full plot of a story in chronological order. Subplots are now logically related to larger plots; relationships among patterns can be ascertained and elucidated.

There is greater interest in themes of control, rules, organization and higher-level domination or submission. These children are more than ever conscious of the differences between boys and girls; they tend to reflect their families' values and sex roles. There is variable interest in talking both with peers and, somewhat sheepishly, with adults about sex. This is a time made colorful by dirty jokes and giggling. Concerns with self-regard and how others regard one are also prominent. Internal morality is relatively well established in an "all good/all bad" polarity, but it is still easy to rationalize transgressions. In fact, along with a greater concern for right and wrong, there is a more sophisticated capacity for rationalizing how to get around the rules. Self-control and the capacity to follow instructions are well established.

The family that provides a secure base from which the child can leave comfortably, and to which the child can be welcomed after school, provides necessary emotional fueling for students. The child from such a family feels free to reach out to other children for play, companionship and reassurance. Girls are more likely to have one or two "best" friends, while boys may name six or seven friends. The successful identifications and comfortable playing with children (usually of the same sex) are very important signs of health.

Moreover, in terms of family tasks, this is the period when families must congeal—become a real group that can do and share together—whether there is one parent or two. Families at this period can do many things together: travel, camp out, join other families in leisure activities or communal projects. At home children should share the everyday chores and can help if a parent is ill. It is a period when children's attachments to and involvement with peers and family members should be about equal.

RISKS

It is obvious that with so much development and learning to accomplish, children at this stage need to be protected from premature initiation into genital sex, from family violence, from pathologic attempts to keep the child tied to home, or from premature independence and too little supervision. The child progressing through grade school deserves any indicated special help with learning problems, mood disorders, hyperactivity, immaturity, excessive fears, and family problems. Teachers and after-school recreation personnel can spot the child who has a special need and can often play the major role in early detection and arranging for intervention. The child who is different for any reason is at social risk with peers, who are at a stage of development where being "like the other kids" is all important.

Other risks are shown by first graders who are unable to sit still, concentrate and process new auditory and hand-eye skill material. Learning to read is a prerequisite in our Western culture, and a satisfactory acquisition of reading skills is one of the most fundamental hallmarks of this life stage. Clearly, children who cannot learn to read may also experience difficulties writing and with word problems in mathematics. These children are at high risk of developing problems with self-esteem.

Children can have difficulty learning to read for many reasons. They may start school already feeling incompetent and/or depressed because of a nonnurturant home. If children feel no sense of past accomplishment, they will lack the motivation to attempt new challenges. They may appear lethargic, distracted or even mentally retarded. A child who has suffered a major loss through death or divorce or because of an illness may lose a year of classroom work while working through the mourning.

A nonreading youngster may need evaluation for hyperactivity. A child who cannot sit at the desk and maintain attention is unable to learn, and can disrupt the entire class and try the teacher's patience.

Children with critical undiagnosed learning disabilities such as dyslexia will continue to be unsuccessful in reading. Leaving such children in large regular classrooms without special help sets up a cycle of failure. Frustrated learning-disabled children are at risk for subsequent depression unless remedial help is provided.

Teachers are aware of these problems and contingencies, but the family provides the emotional climate in which children live, even while at school. If parents are able to convey enthusiasm and pride (without the pressure of too high expectations), the youngster is able to share in their anticipation of a good school experience. Too rigid or harsh views at home can be reflected in a young student's anxiety. Likewise a lack of interest in the child's school progress can also manifest itself in the child's apathy or disrespect at school. On the other hand, there are teachers who may deal poorly or even harshly with some children, in which instances the child needs the family's help and support to cope with the problem. Caretakers must be alert to the possibilities that either system—family or school—can malfunction.

Failure to incorporate rules can seriously handicap a child's socialization progress. This is often first evidenced by a child's inability to play peacefully with peers. Breaking rules in order to win or insisting on having one's own way infuriates other children. They then choose not to play with the "cheater" or "bully." This is an early warning sign to a teacher that a child is having trouble. Possible reasons for the child's failure to follow rules include emotional deprivation and neediness, anger, general immaturity, hyperactivity and lack of comprehension of rules, or familial deficiencies in these respects.

Stereotyped and rigid views about a child's potential, behavior or "goodness" whether at home or at school can be disadvantageous. Commonly, families will "assign" a special role or niche for each child: the "athlete," the "no-good" child, or the "quiet" one who may be expected to stay at home and eventually look after aging parents. These expectations may handicap a child in further maturation and development. The frontline practitioner who gets to know such a family can be in a position to suggest to parents activities or opportunities which can draw out a child's other talents and broaden his or her personality.

Family problems and failure to provide an appropriately secure atmosphere can result in a child's fearfulness or resistance to leaving home. In many school districts, it can be weeks or months before appropriate authorities are notified of prolonged or frequent absences. Sometimes the child's fearfulness is shared or engendered by a parent who really does not mind that the child stays at home. Physical evidence of child abuse may be a reason why youngsters are being kept out of school. Children who are afraid that they will not be able to perform in school may develop headaches or stomach pain so that they can stay home. Home-bound tutoring is not helpful with such a child.

In two-thirds of families with school-age children, the single parent or both parents work outside the home. While economically advantageous, if not necessary, this situation may also pose risks. First, if there are no after-school programs available to the child or children, they may become "latch key waifs." Such unsupervised children and adolescents may feel deprived and/or get into mischief. If the parents work different shifts, this risk can be avoided, but family life may be handicapped by the absence of one parent, especially at suppertime, the prime time for family togetherness and interaction. In view of the increase in biparental employment, age-appropriate after-school programs have become an absolute necessity. Their establishment requires communal and political action supported by professionals.

PREVENTIVE INTERVENTIONS

It is important to recognize that the family and the school are deeply engaged with children's problems at this age. Difficulties can be rooted in either one or both, innate psychobiological and learning handicaps in the child aside. Without integration and coordination of the two systems, risk-reducing and preventive work will fail, no matter where the difficulty originates. Parent-teacher meetings and conferences are important parts of preventive interventions, whether aimed at family difficulties, at school and teaching methods, or at providing some special help for the student. Finally, a preventive program that schools and families should agree to provide and coordinate should include instruction in general health, in health behavior, and in body functions, sexuality included.

Rule-breaking behavior and the resultant ostracism should warn teachers, parents and coaches of a problem in the child or the family or both. Intervention can often be made on the spot by spending extra time with the child, giving parents guidance, or setting up a behavioral program to encourage appropriate interactions with peers. Since working parents often do not have the opportunity to observe their school-age children at play with classmates, feedback from teachers and coaches is essential. Early notice that a child is experiencing too much frustration or is driven to break rules can result in early intervention. Successful adaptation to society requires the ability to follow society rules and accommodate to group activities.

Behavioral treatment approaches involving parents and teacher, often with the help of the pediatrician, are indicated when a student is chronically truant from school. Parents are part of such problems and may feel apprehensive if not guilty when a "sick" child is "ordered" back to school. Such parents may benefit from explanations of the child's and their own fears and concerns. Parental anxiety may keep the child home, and if so, must be addressed helpfully.

In the vignette, Randy's symptoms became evident in his inability to play with his peers. When his coach checked with teachers, he learned that Randy's academic performance was good. However, Randy could not take part in group activities without whining, blaming others for his difficulties, and behaving in a generally immature manner. Because Randy seemed to be going out of his way to call attention to himself, his coach made the effort to discuss this observation with Randy's parents. In this way it was discovered that Randy had no family providing togetherness and cementing the sense of belonging during the week. Although his 15-year-old sister did an adequate job of supervising homework, she was truly incapable of providing the secure and engaged home or leadership needed by a school-age child. Randy was not receiving the minimum nurturance and support or a sense of "being held" that he needed at this period, since his "family" existed only on weekends. Without a solid sense of home and self, it is difficult to venture comfortably into the world of peers.

Randy's teacher and the principal called the mother in for an emergency meeting. They clearly stated the need for a parent in the home during the week. Explanation was offered for why the school felt that Randy's problems stemmed from a lack of support at home. When the mother became indignant and pointed out that the high tuition she paid the school was to provide Randy with not only good academics but a solid after-school program and supervision, the school administrator took a strong stand. She explained that the law required her to report any case of neglect or abuse, and if Randy continued to live in a parentless home, the school would be forced to file a report. Fortunately for Randy, his mother and the school, this pressure convinced the mother of her importance to his welfare. She found a job in their home city and was able to schedule her life so she could be home in the evenings. Randy's behavior in the after-school programs gradually became age-appropriate. His coach heard much less whining and saw much more assertive competitiveness. He was especially pleased to hear the boys talk about the great slumber party Randy had had for his eleventh birthday. Randy had achieved another milestone for his age, appropriate parental leadership was restored, and the crisis resolution reduced risks for further maldevelopment.

REFERENCES

Greenspan, S.I., & Pollock, G.H. (Eds.) (1980). *The course of life. Vol. II. Latency, adolescence and youth.* DHHS Publ. No. (ADM) 80–999. Washington, DC: US Government Printing Office.

Kellam, S.G., Baruch, J.D., Agrawal, K.C., et al. (1975). *Mental health and going to school.* Chicago: University of Chicago Press.

Kohlberg, L. (1974). The development of moral stages: Uses and abuses. Proceedings of the 1973 Conference on Testing Problems. *Educational Testing Services,* 1–8.

Rutter, M., Tizard, J., & Whitmore, K. (1970). *Education, health and behaviour.* London: Longman Group.

Senn, M., & Solnit, A.J. (1968). *Problems in child behavior and development.* Philadelphia: Lea & Febiger.

8

THE ADOLESCENT FAMILY

Sandy was a 15-year-old girl from a middle-class family. Her gym teacher noticed that Sandy had been spending increasing numbers of study hall hours and after-practice time in the gym office. At times shy and awkward around her teacher, Sandy could alternatively pour out 30 minutes of tearful tirades over the injustice of being her parents' daughter. In any given impassioned monologue, Sandy's parents were portrayed as uncaring and uninvolved or nosy, overly strict, too wrapped up in their own professions and too intrusive into her life. She made dramatic statements about how it would serve them right if she ran away, killed herself, or never spoke to them again. Although her good grades remained stable and she maintained several close friends (who also "hated" their parents), life at home had deteriorated into shouting matches, threats and power struggles. As the weeks passed, the gym teacher began to feel a shift in Sandy's mood as she cried more and complained less. There seemed to be a certainty developing that life would always be painful. Then Sandy was grounded by her parents and had to drop out of the team. She continued to show up at the gym office during study halls, but she seemed thinner and more withdrawn.

This vignette includes a few of the many painful experiences that can occur during adolescence. Sandy is not atypical among middle-class teenagers. She experienced the rapid mood swings that allow her to be verbal and expressive on one occasion and restrict her to insecure shyness the next. She despaired that the parents she so loved a short time ago, and who doted on her, now seemed only to yell, criticize and restrict her freedom. She had felt favored over her 11-year-old brother, but now he seemed to be indulged and "getting away with murder." Struggles reemerged as Sandy believed that what she ate, whom she saw, what she wore, and where she went were issues that *she* should determine.

As Sandy did, many adolescents choose an "alternate adult" with whom to talk and identify. This allows the teenager to confide in and develop a trusting relationship with a supportive adult while moving away from the parents. Teachers, counselors, clergy, coaches, youth leaders, and health personnel often find themselves in such a relationship with a young person. The relationship may be the formal one in the guidance or pediatric office, or the "hero worship" on the practice field.

The gym teacher recognized that Sandy was reaching out, and that she was being wooed as a friend, confidant and substitute parent. At first the teacher listened but beyond being available to Sandy found no indication to intervene until Sandy had to leave the team and began losing weight.

The adult who spends time with teenagers needs to be aware of the developmental tasks that are to be achieved during adolescence. These tasks are:

1. The adolescent is involved in a normal seesaw between independence and dependence. The primary relationship with parents needs to be reworked in the transition from childhood to adult personality. In this process a teenager may feel and behave like a demanding, entitled child, and a short time later function in a sophisticated, responsible manner.

2. The adolescent has to become familiar with a constantly changing body. Fluctuating hormone levels effect mood swings, sexual development, growth spurts and acne. The teenager can feel like a stranger in his or her own body.

3. The groundwork for lasting adult sexual relationships is laid during adolescence.

4. A sense of self—defined by values, goals and recreational preferences—is being consolidated.

5. Familial and peer values and behavior standards need to be reconciled, such as peer ideas and enthusiasm with everyday realities, thus necessitating compromises.

6. Career and educational goals and lifestyles are explored and addressed; at least tentative directions are selected.

7. Values, religious beliefs and ethical principles get reexamined by the youth, with some rejected and new ones integrated into an emerging identity.

The alternate adults need to be aware of how an adolescent is coping with these developmental tasks, as well as keep in mind the normal adolescent egocentric perspective. The adolescent is preeminently an actor for an audience of one: him- or herself. At the same time teenagers are acutely aware of other actual or fantasized audiences.

Exposure and physical, social or emotional slights are a preeminent concern for the adolescent. This necessitates privacy and an intense concern over being viewed as defective or deficient. There is great reliance on nonverbal communication. Adolescents are masters at communicating feelings through facial expression, voice tone and inflection, telegraphic, affect-laden words, nuances of gaze, body posture, and movements. This may partly be the result of adolescents' insecurity about their ability to articulate as adults, and partly an effective way of identifying their own "style" as separate from the parents' manners and mannerisms.

Adolescence is real life, but it is also rehearsal. The adolescent, especially the young adolescent from ages 11 to 15, is constantly reexperiencing his or her body and relearning to live in and use it in new ways. The adolescent is developing new, emerging cognitive styles, new language usage and new social experiences, and he or she is engaging in a long series of rehearsals and refinements while experimenting with competent, confident and adult behavior. This is not to say that adolescence is not a period of play, nor does it minimize the reality of life for adolescents, but much of what they are doing at times is trying out or acting out various roles, attitudes, expressions or modes of thinking. Such tentative behavior helps them to see what fits and what does not fit. In this context the adolescent's fidgetiness, lounging, lolling, giggling, posing and posturing are part of managing affect and energy discharge. It also involves dealing with the acute somesthetic and kinesthetic sensations that go with the "newness" of the emerging adult body shape and body image. Adolescents frequently ask themselves in observing their own behavior, "Is this the right way? The 'cool' or the sexy way? The smart way? The adult way?"

Adolescence may be divided into two periods: early adolescence, from ages 11 to 15, and late adolescence, from ages 16 to 20. It is during the early period—with the greatest biopsychosocial change—that the adolescent is much more diffuse, fluid and generally more labile in terms of the developmental tasks. It is also the time when adolescents are more vulnerable to stressors within the family or developmental risks carried over from childhood.

The body holds center stage for 11- to 15-year-old adolescents. It should be noted that this is not only or necessarily sexual, but the body intrudes upon the awareness of the adolescent as a preoccupation, consternation and concern as well as a source of satisfaction and enjoyment. Sexual issues may be central at this time, but issues of dependency and autonomy emerge as major matters and are worked out in different ways from those in earlier life cycle stages.

Cognitive maturation and development bear directly on educational achievement; moral judgment and the gradually consolidating sense of identity determine the ability to set boundaries between the individual and the peer group. Educational and athletic pursuits are particularly crucial, for they relate to sources of or threats to self-esteem and stimulate future goal-oriented behavior.

The extension of time perspective—retrospectively and prospectively—is a significant psychosocial process that develops at this stage. This sense of a personal past and a future influences adolescent thoughts about self, family and friends, allowing for reinterpretation of one's sense of self in the contexts of family and of larger sociocultural systems. Space is another expanding reality as the adolescent's daily life may involve a school at a greater distance from home, requiring the use of public transportation or an automobile.

The age of 16 (with a standard deviation of one year) usually brings the adolescent to adult body size and shape. Cognitive development with the capacity for more generalized abstract thinking has emerged and is being consolidated, along with an overinvestment in ideas and the achievability of ideals. Modulation of affect and behavior is more finely tuned. Capacity for using the mind as a problem-solving instrument and for cognitive rehearsal has become more integrated. Impulsivity is generally better managed. Sexual information, attitudes and behavior are somewhat more integrated.

Confrontation, reexamination and the development and formation of values different from those of the parents are major issues of adolescent development, particularly in the later stages. These issues of autonomy and dependency relate to the whole area of cognitive-affective social relationships, including sexual awareness and exploration.

The issue of privacy is important. The adolescent is preoccupied with privacy of his or her own room, of communications, of the body, with at times increased concern about modesty. At other times quite the opposite occurs: Flaunting of the body may be rather provocative, at times even exhibitionistic, but not necessarily sexually motivated. The privacy that the adolescent becomes aware of and treasures, protects and defends with great passion is privacy of the mind. Many adolescents become solitary, more inward persons, at times because of confusion and concern about what is going on inside, at times because they are anxious, even depressed, about what is happening in their interpersonal lives. Privacy of thought, feelings and actions is a major concern and often defended at all costs. Ironically this coincides with parents' greater interest in open communication with their adolescent child, which is generally encouraged by experts and the media. Parents may feel confused, frustrated and even guilty when all their attempts in this regard go awry. The confusions stem from adolescents' moodiness, which may seem like a plea for help or contact, but then they are less available and less communicative, particularly around personal, emotionally charged matters.

In many instances, by age 16 adolescents and their parents have generally shared the outline of the new social contract between them, even though many of the specific details of policy and procedure remain to be worked out, sometimes with equanimity and sometimes with pain and distressful conflict. The adolescent has become more future oriented, as he or she is much more concerned with shaping school and after-school experiences toward a near or distant future goal of job or further education.

PARENTING THE ADOLESCENT

Adolescents work out the identity issues, independence/dependence conflicts and future orientation within the context of their families. Teenagers need—but may not want or seek—attentive support, interest, guidance, structure and limits as well as reinforcement from the adults in their family. Structure is needed to provide something solid against which the adolescent can push; limits prevent premature rupture from the family. Wisdom and judgment as well as tact allow the parent to adjust the structure and limit setting, provide leadership and guidance, and pace the growth and development of the young person.

Some families are more able to provide consistent supportive attention to teenagers. In evaluating the family, consideration needs to be given to issues of roles, relationships between spouses and between parents and children, intergenerational boundaries, ways of communicating and problem solving, and intrafamilial dynamics and development in a multigenerational context. External stressors acting on the family can be socioeconomic, such as job loss or even promotion of the wage earner requiring family relocation and new schools and the need to acquire new friends.

Neither previous parental successes or failures nor the parents' recollections of their teenage experience provide an adequate map for the challenges which adolescence presents. If the prior family stage went well, transition to the adolescent stage may be comfortable, although unexpected issues do arise. Parents need to promote the child's autonomy and yet support dependency as required, setting appropriate limits and providing clarity about values and expectations. The parents need to be available and initiate contact despite some of the adolescent's resistance and aloofness, while also respecting the privacy of mind and other domains of the adolescent in peer relationships.

Parents and adults are generally concerned with the issue of limits for adolescent behavior, but the adolescents themselves are more concerned with boundaries. The issue of privacy is a predominant value and one way of establishing the boundaries in many different arenas of life. Parents need to be clear and in agreement about nonnegotiable aspects of family life, but must tolerate the need for renegotiating the social contract between themselves and the child who is striving to leave childhood behind and prepare for adulthood. Parents need to know that the first three to four years of adolescence—the time of the greatest biological, emotional and social changes—can be stormy, more fluid and stressful for the family.

In discussing the family context in which the adolescent lives, the life-stage of the parents must be considered. Young parents, often still vigorous athletically and active socially, may feel closer to their adolescent children, but may also feel more competitive. As a result they may act in overly strict or overly permissive ways—stances that may be determined by their own adolescent experience and responses to their own parents. Younger parents may not provide the limits or mature judgment that the adolescent may need at this time, possibly because the parents are likely to be preoccupied and intensely involved in their own careers and social development. They may be less alert to the adolescent's particular experience or stresses and may find that their own priorities take precedence over attention to the adolescent's developmental needs and stresses. Middle-aged parents are likely more settled in careers, but increased responsibility in job and career may be an added stress for the wage earners, making it harder to attend to the needs of the spouse and of adolescent and younger children.

Two-career families are common in this age group, and the mother who may have been more available for her younger children may now cause an adolescent child to feel neglected or abandoned. Partly because of adolescents' intense insistence on privacy and their peer group orientation, popular dogma has held that parents ought to "stay out of the adolescent's life." This undue "respect" for an adolescent's privacy can have unfortunate and even disastrous consequences. Despite overt claims to the contrary, adolescents need and covertly expect parental interest, availability and, in varying degrees, expressions of authority. This is particularly true for the adolescent under the age of 16. The risk of an adolescent feeling abandoned and left out can be inadvertently rationalized by parents who justify the pursuits of their own interests by saying that the children do not want intrusion.

Adolescent children can place new stresses on parental identities and the parental relationship. Parents who are in their mid-40s and 50s encounter biological as well as psychological stresses. Men at this age are at increased risk for coronary artery disease, hypertension and other chronic and recurrent illnesses. Stresses on the job or in the marriage may lead them to substance abuse. At times stresses in the marriage may lead to more open conflicts, separations, infidelities. Women at this period are premenopausal to menopausal, with all of the attendant biological and psychological stresses. Parents may envy the younger, vigorous adolescent about to begin life, when they may feel they are over their peak physically, sexually, socially and in their careers. Thus, parents may intentionally or inadvertently deal with their adolescent children in a jealous, rivalrous or demeaning way. Their increased attempts at control of the adolescent may not be in the service of helping the young person set reasonable limits and exercise good judgment. Allowing increased autonomy may signal to parents the end of an era for themselves as individuals, as a married couple, and of tangible parental tasks.

Adolescents may become aware of interpersonal difficulties between parents, which they had not perceived earlier or which were not as obvious or intense previously. Adolescents aware of chronic or recurrent marital stress between their parents may respond with anxiety or depression, or may exploit the conflict and remain caught up in the family stresses instead of coping with the experience of adolescence. Adolescents may secondarily attract the parents' attention away from the parental conflict by being distraught or by misbehaving. Caretakers need to be alert to substance abuse among adolescents, to rapid entry into sexual activity, and to adolescents who never stay home or else withdraw or isolate themselves. While such manifestations or problems may be part of the adolescent experience per se, such behaviors may also indicate family problems.

RISKS

Changes occurring during puberty and adolescence may highlight previously existing risk factors. Those children who were clinically disturbed prior to adolescence are more vulnerable to the emergence of psychosocial disturbance during this dynamic period of life. Risk factors that can alert caretakers to a potentially vulnerable adolescent include:

1) Extremely rigid families with closed, impermeable boundaries;
2) Chronic illness in child or family;
3) Divorce or chronic marital disruption;
4) Previous learning disability or attention deficit disorder;
5) Repeated social failures in grade school;
6) Siblings involved in antisocial activities.

Adolescents offer many varied behavioral signals when they are experiencing emotional crisis. A list of adolescents' behavioral signals of risks for maldevelopment or maladjustment is presented in Table 4.

PREVENTIVE INTERVENTIONS

It is a challenge to help adolescents "open up" and share feelings with adults, even when an at-risk adolescent initiates a contract with an alternate adult. Even more difficulty can be experienced when a caring adult approaches a young person who appears troubled. Developmental issues of privacy, boundaries and independence often limit an adolescent's communications with a concerned adult. Frequently adolescents' first response to a question about their lives is: "It's okay" or "It's not bad" or "It's all right." If one accepts that response as definitive, the session with the adolescent

TABLE 4
At-Risk Behavioral Signals in Adolescence

1. Need for street drugs or alcohol in order to avoid coping with school, recreation or sex.
2. Sudden drop in school grades.
3. Social isolation. No friends, dates or phone calls.
4. Undue risk taking. Reckless car driving, use of tobacco, use of street drugs, unprotected intercourse, solitary hitchhiking, compulsive sexual activity.
5. Preoccupation with persons who have committed suicide or become notorious for antisocial acts.
6. Running away.
7. Suicide "threat."
8. Dramatic changes in weight or sleep patterns.
9. Unremitting sadness.
10. Sexual encounters with younger children.
11. Habitual lying even when not needed to avoid punishment.
12. Truancy.
13. Teenage pregnancy.
14. Fantasy life which consistently intrudes upon learning, relationships or sleep.
15. Escape via religious conversion in a way that precludes experiencing normal adolescent questioning and searching.
16. Membership in asocial or destructive gangs.

will be short, unproductive and frustrating. The helpful adult's response to the adolescent's rather noncommital or indifferent initial reaction can be: "Well, let's hear about the okay part and then about the not-so-okay part." The caring adult could also respond: "I'll bet you'd like to be better than just okay. What could be better if you could have things the way you want?"

Adolescents' explicit denial or alleged indifference to a question or suggestion, especially if offered gratuitously, should alert the professional that the item does matter. "My girl friend says . . ." or "My friend's brother heard . . ." or "Lots of kids worry about . . ., but I don't" are cues to what is troubling the teenager. Sometimes teenagers will be more explicit and say, "Have you heard about this lotion?" that relates to some cosmetic, body building, sexual or developmental aspect. If one takes these overtures as queries or expressions of concerns, one can then follow up, inform, reassure, educate, correct.

Adults should avoid getting into long contests over silence. Adolescents may take silence as an accusation or disinterest or a challenge and merely prove that they can outlast the interviewer, which they always can. Questions like "Why?" should be avoided as they are challenging. It is better to ask longer, more ambiguous questions like "What do you make of that?" or "What were you thinking when you decided to do that?" Many adolescents do not have the opportunity to have a significant, relatively unbiased adult take them seriously and listen to them.

Adolescents rehearse a variety of roles and skills in preparation for adulthood and often are painfully self-conscious about their relative inexperience or lack of ability to talk confidently and fluently with an adult. Therefore, they are often laconic, telegraphic, and use many nonspecific fillers such as "you know," "okay," or "cool." In addition to being space fillers, these are affective or evaluative statements or statements of release. They are not necessarily content- or cognition-specific; but with help the adolescent can tease out the specific content, ideas and attitudes.

It is essential to keep in mind that adolescents are learning how to be familiar and comfortable with a different body, and also learning different cognitive, linguistic and social ways of behaving. They are rehearsing, but it is also very real. Parents and other adults help them rehearse, practice and live just by listening and talking. That alone is extremely significant, independent of the content of the conversation. Adolescents need to hide from themselves and from others that they feel awkward, unskilled or in need of practice. Exposure of these insecurities is to be avoided for they will be defended against at all costs. It is important, therefore, not to confront adolescents with their awkwardness or discomfort, unless one is very sure of the relationship and has some specific therapeutic goal or benefit in mind by doing so.

In general, dealing with adolescents in groups is preferable and recommended when they are taught about dating, sexuality and substance abuse. School clinics should be available for adolescents with questions about, or problems with, these issues. Providing fertility control information in such settings is controversial, as is the dispensation of birth control agents, but both have been found effective in reducing uprotected sexual intercourse and unwanted pregnancy (Zelnick & Kim, 1982).

It is also instructive for high school students to work in nurseries or daycare centers, getting first-hand experience with parenting tasks and responsibilities. Ideally such programs should take place in, or be attached to, high schools, both for staff and students who already have babies and need the service as well as being of service to the community.

In the vignette, the gym teacher was offered the challenge and privilege of being an active listener to Sandy. The teacher did not have to seek out Sandy; the student chose her as an alternate adult. For months the teacher listened to the intense emotion and conveyed her concern, liking and respect for Sandy. The teacher recognized that although there was a lot of pain, Sandy was continuing in her developmental tasks of education, relationships and future orientation. Need for active intervention appeared when, in desperation, perhaps, Sandy's parents responded to her behavior by restricting her from team sports, which were a wholesome and necessary outlet for this girl, and when Sandy responded with withdrawal and undue weight loss. Having invested many hours in getting to know Sandy, her teacher recognized these risk signals and decided to tell Sandy that she was concerned.

Considering Sandy a responsible individual at risk, possibly for anorexia nervosa, her teacher offered her several options which allowed Sandy control. The gym teacher suggested that Sandy ask her parents to come with her to speak with the gym teacher or school counselor. Another option was for the gym teacher to call the parents directly with Sandy's permission. She also offered to give Sandy the names of therapists she might want to contact before or after talking with her parents. The teacher's message was "You have many options for getting some help with your relationships at home and I care enough to support (and push) you in choosing

one of these options." It is important to allow adolescents to participate in decisions concerning their health and welfare. Even if they
opt for a plan not the first choice of the frontline practitioner, it is
more likely to succeed than if the adolescent feels coerced. The
ideal plan here would be a conference with parents and child,
possibly followed by family therapy if indicated.

REFERENCES

Abramse, A.F., & Morrison, P.A. (1988). Teenagers willing to consider single
    parenthood: Who is at greatest risk? *Family Planning Perspectives, 20,* 13–18.
Anthony, E.J. (1970). The reactions of parents to adolescents and to their behavior.
    In E.J. Anthony & T. Benedek (Eds.), *Parenthood: Its psychology and psychopathology.*
    Boston: Little, Brown.
Aro, H., Paronen, O., & Aro, S. (1987). Psychosomatic symptoms among 14–16
    year-old Finnish students. *Social Psychiatry, 22,* 171–176.
Benn, S. (1987). Connecticut teen wellness check. *Connecticut Health Bulletin, 99,*
    169–172.
Bruch, H. (1980). The family as background to obesity. In J.G. Howells (Ed.),
    International Journal of Family Psychiatry, 1, 77–94.
Campbell, I.A., Breibmayer, B., & Ranny, C.T. (1986). Disadvantaged single teenage
    mothers and their children: Consequences of free educational day care.
    Family Relations, 35, 63–68.
Dryfoos, J.G. (1988). School-based health clinics: Three years experience. *Family
    Planning Perspectives, 20,* 193–200.
Fairfax County Public Schools. (1987). *Adolescent suicide prevention program.* Fairfax,
    VA: Author.
Furstenberg, F.F., & Crawford, A.G. (1980). Social implications of teenage child-
    bearing. In P.B. Smith & D.M. Mumford (Eds.), *Adolescent pregnancy: Perspec-
    tives for the health professional* (pp. 48–76). Boston: G.K. Hall.
Greenspan, S.I., & Pollock, G.H. (Eds.) (1980). *The course of life. Vol. II: Latency,
    adolescence and youth.* NIMH. DHHS Publ. No. (ADM) 80–999. Washington,
    DC: US Government Printing Office.
Group for the Advancement of Psychiatry. (1978). *Power and authority in adolescence.*
    New York: GAP Publications.
Group for the Advancement of Psychiatry. (1986). *Crisis of Adolescence. Teenage
    pregnancy: Impact on adolescent development.* New York: Brunner/Mazel.
Hanson, S.L., Myers, D.E., & Ginsburg, A. (1984). The role of responsibility and
    knowledge in reducing teen out-of-wedlock childbearing. *Journal of Marriage
    and Family Relations, 49,* 241–256.
Holman, N., & Arcus, M. (1987). Helping adolescent mothers and their children:
    An integrated multiagency approach. *Family Relations, 36,* 119–128.

International Planned Parenthood Federation. (1984). *Adolescent fertility.* London: Author.

Klerman, L.V., & Jekel, J.F. (1973). *School age mothers. Problems, programs and policy.* Hamden, CT: The Shoe String Press.

Offer, D., & Offer, J.B. (1975). *From teenage to young manhood.* New York: Basic Books.

Rakkolainen, V. (1977). Onset of psychosis. A clinical study of 68 cases. *University of Turku Finland Series D, 7.*

Zelnick, M., & Kim, Y.J. (1982). Sex education and its association with teenage sexual activity, pregnancy and contraceptive use. *Family Planning Perspectives, 14,* 117–126.

9

EMANCIPATION AND EARLY ADULTHOOD

Mrs. C, 56 years old, was quite voluble during her appointment with her doctor. She described her puzzlement about
her 24-year-old son, Bill. "He was always such a nice boy—
never gave us any trouble." She reported that for the past year,
she and her husband had wanted to sell the family home and
buy a condominium, since Bill was the last child. They had
not planned to take him along, but they wondered if he could
make it on his own. After high school he spent two years in
college while living at home, dropped out twice, then gave up
college. He had worked only sporadically since then. Mrs. C
said that he seemed content to hang around the house and
see his friends on weekends. When she asked him about
getting his own place, he always responded that it would be a
financial hardship and that he was still looking for the "right
thing." Mrs. C added, "I guess we've never pushed him much,
but why doesn't he have more spunk."

The doctor sensed that the young man had at least temporarily
"lost his way" in moving to a more mature stage of development. It
was not at all clear, however, what could be done about the situation
because the person complaining was not Bill but his mother;
moreover, it appeared at least superficially that Bill was content
with the status quo. There was no mention of a girlfriend or talk
about marriage. Was this Mrs. C's blind spot, or did it say something
about Bill's level of psychological maturity and unreadiness for an
intimate relationship? Lastly, the physician had to consider the
mother's intent in sharing her dissatisfactions so readily. Did she
expect an answer or solution or did she want the doctor to talk Bill

into becoming more independent? Simply telling Mrs. C to "get your son to go to a counselor," although probably good advice, might not be very helpful since Bill's reluctance to address his situation might well be part of the problem.

Instead, the physician tried to find out more about the family and, within the limits of role and time constraints, planned to use this knowledge to suggest different family interventions tailored to this family's particular style and organization. Questions in the doctor's mind about this mother's story might be divided into three parts: about the family, about the son, and about the practitioner-patient relationship. Had the parents put off enjoying their own life until they had launched all of their children? Did they now resent the last son's intrusion into their life plan? Had the parents seen Bill as the baby of the family and encouraged his dependency? Did they now have to live with a son who had difficulty separating from them? The statement "I guess we've never pushed him much" suggests that the family had possibly transmitted doubts to Bill about whether he could really ever make it on his own. Possibly the spouses were concerned about a successful married life without parenthood tasks.

It seemed from the mother's description that Bill was quite content to stay at home and be cared for. Was this really true? Perhaps Mrs. C. did not perceive Bill's inner turmoil, or perhaps she sensed it but denied it to herself. Casting about for a direction might be a sign of searching for an identity. This is often accompanied by some distress or dissatisfaction, but in this case that seemed to be missing. Bill was "content" to hang around the house. Did this reflect some early sign of a more serious disturbance such as schizophrenia, or was it Bill's reaction to his parents' ambivalence at separating from their last child?

The concerns expressed by Mrs. C about her son embody many of the issues and problems frequently associated with the transition from adolescence to young adulthood. A child's life has been intimately tied to the family, but now the journey toward real autonomy begins—a journey begun, in a sense, at birth. The first full-time permanent job, college away from home, a circle of friends, a continuing sexual involvement, all require a capacity for more independent functioning than may have been experienced heretofore. The ability to meet these varied psychosocial demands will, of course, depend in great measure on how well previous life experiences, in and out of the family, have helped prepare for these opening scenes in the real-life drama in the grown-up world. Often clues to a young adult's readiness to assume his or her place in that world may be gleaned from some sense of how completely he or she has emerged from adolescence.

If young people over 18 living at home are still engaged in continuing conflict with the family around such issues as dating, doing chores, or choice of friends, they are apt to be less well prepared to establish a satisfactory life pattern when they do have the opportunity to be physically free of parental controls. They may remain so enmeshed in the struggle to either comply with or rebel against parental constraints and values that they achieve very little progress in establishing their own values, modes and standards of behavior. If the issues continue to be whether they are their "own person" rather than what their parents expect or need them to be, their emergence into the adult world may leave them dazed and uncertain about who they are, where they want to be, or what they want to be doing.

If, while still attached to the family base, adolescents have been able to find a comfortable niche with neighborhood and/or high school peers, the task of making a place for themselves in a college or work situation will follow easily. Within such peer groups, patterns of social and sexual intimacy will begin to emerge. Views of the self as a productive, competent, lovable, worthwhile person will be confirmed and consolidated, or the individual will be assailed by doubts, uncertainty and apprehension. The resulting impairment of self-esteem and confidence may seriously interfere with the individual's initial experience at college, seeking or beginning a first full-time job, or establishing a satisfactory "grown-up" love affair. If these problems arise, young adults are unlikely to appeal for help in the company of their parents. Even if they are still living at home, their need for assistance and their parents' concerns about them tend to surface independently.

Indications that a family may be less than fully supportive of a young adult's efforts to separate may be discerned from how well parents have made their own adjustments to life without tangible parental tasks. Parents whose whole life and energies have centered around the care of children may experience an almost intolerable sense of loss. This is the well-known "empty nest" syndrome, which may put them at risk for depression. Other parents may actually feel relieved as the time for the last child's departure approaches. Such parents support their children's moves toward separation. However, some families precipitously push children out with inadequate preparation and little real encouragement. A few principles and guidelines may serve as reminders for the frontline practitioners who see late adolescents, young adults, and their families:

1. To become autonomous persons, young adults ultimately have to achieve psychosocial separation from their family. Although often this will entail actual physical separation, the emotional distance is critical. Some young adults move far away physically but fail to leave home emotionally. Others may, for practical or cultural reasons, continue to live at home while single, yet gain their psychosocial autonomy.

2. Becoming an independent person involves a capacity to direct and govern one's life, striving toward productive citizenship, being capable of economic survival and communal involvement. The choice of a job, college, technical training, running a household, or some less traditional path may not be as significant as how the choices are made and implemented. Choices dictated primarily by compliance with or rebellion against parental ideals usually do not augur well for a productive career or a gratifying growth experience. People in such situations represent a risk for continued dependence-seeking situations. To accept assistance and advice from those in a position to help need not impair the young adult's sense of achievement and independence, but an adamant posture of refusing all

aid and an insistence on "doing it all myself" does not necessarily connote autonomy.

3. With the absence of direct parental supervision, the issue of young adults' sexual identity and choice of close friends or sexual partners become matters primarily determined by themselves. The relative absence of external limitations and constraints may be conducive to an accelerated period of growth and maturation or may intensify conflicts and issues of sexual identity and intimacy not adequately resolved during childhood or adolescence. Many young adults who have not resolved issues of sexual identity, choice of friends, or lifestyle while living under the parental roof do manage to do so when they have the opportunity to experiment and explore options in a life which is primarily peer oriented. College or work away from home may provide an easier transition than remaining within the parental sphere. The goal for some life space of their own, however, is ideally shared by both generations whether they live together or not.

Although emancipation from parents and family of origin is often demarcated by such tangible changes in life status as entering college or a job, progression into adulthood is less clearly delineated. It evolves around consolidation of career or work and establishment of intimate relationships initiated during the emancipatory phase. It may lead to marriage, the formation of a new family, childrearing, and movement toward lifetime peaks of health, energy and work. Usually it also includes a growing role and participation in one's community.

As young adults become autonomous, they will often have achieved some type of intimacy with a sexual partner and a lifestyle satisfying to them. Young adults launched in career or job, with their own marital or family life established and adjusted in their community, are considered to be "on their own" in this society. How well they continue to cope with the variety of issues and problems with which life presents them will be determined not only by their own inner resources, competence and health, but also by the supports available to them from the social context in which they live. If they are members of some form of extended family within a closely knit community, such supports may be an integral part of their lives. On the other hand, the single adult or small nuclear family living in relative isolation in an urban or suburban environment may be hard put to know where to turn when they encounter expectable stresses or crises.

The major family task at this stage of the life cycle is to help the young achieve the self-sufficiency to carry on as the next generation in their society. The departure of young people from their family of origin affects the entire system. Parents may mourn or take satisfaction and solace to have a son or daughter launched, be that into college, job, military service or marriage. If the choice the young person makes does not seem suitable or constructive to the parents, they are prone to mourn or to enter a stage of prolonged conflict and struggle with the offspring. Of course, there can also be parental disagreement about such matters, which may be relatively new for the spouses, or just another chapter in long-standing marital discord.

If there are siblings left at home, they are also affected by the departure, whether it be an actual leaving or an emotional and psychosocial separation. Younger children are apt to miss a big brother or older sister playing with them or giving them attention. The children who stay at home can also feel relieved if there was much rivalry among siblings, but they also usually feel envious. Intense sibling rivalry often bespeaks inadequate parenting, and if so, the stay-at-home siblings may then become more involved in parental difficulties—the previous "buffer" having departed.

The supportive and caring family will acknowledge their collective sadness, mourn together and reorganize into a smaller group after the loss. A sibling's successful emancipation and departure also serves as a model for the younger ones. Departure of the last child may be especially difficult for the parents as well as for the "baby." The latter has had more support, caring and companionship than the older siblings. This could enhance his or her eagerness to depart also, or make the transition more difficult than the ones experienced by the older children.

RISKS

The process of identity formation needs to be consolidated during this period of emancipation. When this process is not going well, the risk of identity diffusion arises, and there are likely to be difficulties in the individual's work or school life and/or in the ability to establish intimate and satisfying social and sexual relationships. These risks can lead to further maladjustments and to mental illness.

Whether expressed explicitly, unresolved identity issues frequently emerge after young adults begin college or while seeking or starting a job. For others, long-standing unresolved issues may become manifest as alarming symptoms with the move to an adult role. Any evaluation should determine the duration of the problem and connection, if any, to changes in the individual's life situation.

In college concerns about study habits may be explicitly related to the amount of work required, the absence of daily assignments, the distractions of campus social life or of the dormitory environment. Uncertainties about a new job may raise doubts about one's adequacy, about making mistakes or managing one's one budget, and about everyday living. Doubts about self-esteem may be phrased in terms of concern over appearance, clothes, attractiveness, and comparing oneself unfavorably with others in new peer groups. Conflicts over values may appear in connection with such matters as use of drugs and alcohol, sexual activity, and the use of contraception or adherence to religious principles. Young adults may ask for help in coping with situations never encountered or considered in their families of origin.

Complaints about lack of friends may represent a critical point in the progressive withdrawal of a frightened schizoid individual. Problems in work performance may be related to an unacknowledged growing dependence on alcohol or drugs. Risks for serious disturbance such as homosexual conflicts or impending psychotic disorganization may underlie apparently simple requests for advice on sexual matters or career changes.

Other risks are more reflective of our current social arrangements than a product of the young adult's own makeup. Extended postgraduate education may involve prolonged economic dependence on parents or other indebtedness which may impede social maturity, such as postponement of initiating a family. Under such circumstances, young adults who are capable of more autonomous functioning may feel forced into roles they find demeaning and not commensurate with their competence and maturity. Counseling for such young adults, their families, or both may enable all concerned to devise working arrangements which may help weather such stresses and limit the risk level.

Experience in therapeutic work with young adults and their families has demonstrated that risks to emotional health frequently concern "unfinished business" with a parent. Whether or not one engages or can engage the parent in the work of resolving such issues, young individuals at risk must be helped to overcome such emotional hang-ups. Psychotherapy may be indicated to help some of these individuals complete developmental tasks. In such instances the practitioner must establish a relationship that will facilitate appropriate referral.

Other indications that the transition to adulthood is not going well may be signaled as difficulties in keeping a job or progressing in one's career, repeated failure to establish intimate social and sexual relationships, or in loneliness and isolation. Later risk indicators involve concerns about inability to carry out family responsibilities or fears that one may never have a family of one's own. Drug or alcohol abuse and frequent or recurrent somatic complaints are indicators of trouble because they usually serve to avoid painful issues or personal growth.

PREVENTIVE INTERVENTIONS

The caretakers or professionals who might encounter individuals in early adulthood are found in areas central to this stage: college, graduate school, work and marriage. In college a faculty member or counselor might be the first one to whom a student turns. If difficulties are manifested at work, there may be an employee assistance plan or personnel department where counseling is available. Marriage in a church usually includes discussions with clergy about the decision and associated life issues. A physician, as in the vignette, may become the person turned to, especially if he or she has known the family for some time.

After some time on a first job, young people may become overwhelmed with doubts about the wisdom of their choice, their competence, or their future. Rather than focusing on the more remote origins of the individual's anxiety, it may often be more useful first to make a referral to a career-counseling program. Some young adults, particularly in middle-class circles, will respond to difficulties by seeking out a mental health practitioner on their own. Others live in circumstances that neither are conducive to nor encourage such initiative, and where help is not easily found. Many disadvantaged youths live in communities in which large numbers of the young men and women have been ill-prepared by their meager educational experiences for the world of work. Their opportunities for employment are poor and the jobs offered are frequently at a level above their underdeveloped abilities.

Entering into marriage and starting a family as a way to adulthood are precarious ventures. Young adults thus handicapped and stressed manifest their symptoms in welfare offices, hospital clinics, family agencies, or in conflicts with the law. It is crucial that workers and professionals involved with such people be aware of the dire realities and their devastating impact on young people and their families. Unfortunately, many caseworkers in agencies such as welfare departments are neither equipped nor expected to consider personal welfare beyond the determination of clients' eligibility for benefits, leaving the long-range risks unattended. Hospital clinics may do little more than alleviate somatic symptoms, often engendered by overwhelming stress, and a family court may have to limit its assistance to protecting the troubled children of beleaguered parents. Nevertheless, social agencies are in the center of opportunity to identify such risks and prevent further mental and social dysfunction.

Risk reduction and prevention require guidance, counseling, education and possibly therapeutic measures designed to improve the individual's coping capacity, and to forestall pathologic developments. In some settings, preventive educational programs concerning such issues may be offered to the population of a given institution, work setting, or the public at large. When a person in such settings asks for advice or help, it may often be neither acceptable nor feasible to engage in the kind of extensive history taking or clinical evaluation needed to determine the nature and severity of the problem. If individuals do not present themselves in such a way as to invite a more probing evaluation, the caretaker may be well advised to limit the response to the manifest issues presented. The ability of young adults to utilize guidance, counseling or educational assistance may reflect their readiness to proceed with personal growth, sometimes despite significant underlying disturbance. If the nature of the difficulties does require more than informational assistance, but more help is refused, the relationship established may permit eventual consideration of more covert issues by the young adult and the frontline practitioner, possibly facilitating referral to a specialist.

In the vignette, Bill's parents wanted to sell the family home and move to a smaller place. In doing so they would define their parental boundary more sharply. By insisting on remaining at home and because of his difficulty in starting his own separate life, Bill was interfering with that boundary change. Perhaps, however, his parents were allowing him to do so without really realizing the implications for their future life or needs or their own possible unconscious resistance to such change. Which parent was the leader in this family, and were both committed to the contemplated move? What was the family's style in expression or tolerance of affect? How did they handle feelings of love, closeness, resentment, jealousy and anger? The mother presented a rather bland picture of Bill. Was he really this way, or was this a family that could not easily handle strong feelings and thus tended to ignore or deny them? The C family may have difficulty in "letting go" of the last child, giving him an ambivalent message about what they expected of him. Mrs. C says of her son, "I guess we never pushed him enough" and "He was always a nice boy and never gave us any trouble." Such statements should alert the practitioner to the risk of a continued vested interest of the family to maintain Bill as a semidependent person in the household. If this was so, then Bill was "at risk" for psychological conflict or developmental delays in this emancipation phase of the life cycle.

Communication did seem to be a problem, as mother knew very little about what was really going on with her 24-year-old son. Was this an example of the usual family communication style? Perhaps the parents were, without being aware of it, discouraging the very communication they sought. For example, they may have felt that demonstration of parental interest would be seen as an intrusion, or they could be quickly moving to a "lecture" in their discussion with Bill rather than giving him space to tell his side.

After getting some sense of the family, the practitioner was in a much better position to make specific suggestions. In this case the doctor intervened as follows:

1. He felt that boundaries were a problem and encouraged the parents to respect their own needs more and set firmer limits with their son.

2. He supported the mother and let her know that it was "all right" to discuss her fears or angry feelings with her son and to hear his, which might clear the air and allow the family to communicate about the issues.

3. Since the parents had always promoted Bill's dependence on them, his mother was helped to see that this was not a "failure" but a parental response which had been appropriate earlier in Bill's life and that a different response was necessary to help Bill now.

Throughout this more informed discussion with the mother, the doctor was open to seeing other family members and Bill, should he be willing. If the initial intervention did not help, or further information revealed that Bill showed more psychological disturbance or lack of age-appropriate behavior than at first seemed the case, the physician would consider referring Bill to a mental health professional. Lastly, through his earlier contacts the doctor became aware that leadership in this family fell primarily upon the mother, possibly because she sought it, or because the father had eschewed it, or both. This could have affected Bill, who seemed to lack purpose and motivation to become a "leader" for himself, having lacked a strong male figure for identification. Prevention of further passivity and pathology would require therapeutic intervention aiming toward effective masculine identification on Bill's part, as well as vocational counseling to explore Bill's employability or need for further training. As it turned out, Bill did need the latter, but not the former, and, as he explained to the physician, whom he was quite willing to see, Bill wished his mother to "get off my back." Every time he tried to move away, his mother found reasons why it was not "practical" or economically possible. His father did not dispute the mother's pronouncement, but Bill suspected he did not really agree with her. After the three met together with the doctor, they each could make a shift: The father overtly began to support Bill, the mother really began to prepare for a move by the couple, and Bill entered vocational training and planned to live by himself once the house was sold.

REFERENCES

Baruch, G., & Gunn, J.B. (Eds.) (1984). *Women in mid-life.* New York: Plenum Press.

Comer, J.P. (1985). The hidden costs of unemployment. *New York Times,* June 9.

Cooney, T.M., Smeyer, M.A., Hagestad, G.O., & Klock, R. (1982). Parental divorce in young adulthood: Some preliminary findings. *American Journal of Orthopsychiatry, 66,* 470–477.

Karl, S.E, Gore, S., & Cobbs, S. (1975). The experience of losing a job: Reported changes in health, symptoms and illness behavior. *Psychosomatic Medicine, 37,* 106.

Kraus, A.S., & Lilienfeld, A.M. (1959). Some epidemiological aspects of the high mortality in a young widowed group. *Journal of Chronic Diseases, 10,* 207.

Stierlin, H. (1972). *Separating parents and adolescents.* New York: New York Times Books.

10

THE MIDLIFE FAMILY

EARLY MIDDLE LIFE

> Mary G, age 41, burst into tears one day on a routine visit for
> her Pap smear. She felt so alone after almost 20 years of
> marriage to John. Unhappy in her marriage, she complained
> that John seemed to "enjoy having a beer with the boys after
> work" more than being with her. They led almost separate
> lives with the only common areas of interest centering around
> the children, whose care he left almost completely to her. She
> was annoyed at his continued close ties to his own family and
> the fact that he still seemed to have to turn to his mother for
> advice first. Mrs. G had wondered if there was another woman
> but gradually rejected this idea, concluding, "That's just the
> way he is."

The physician was taken aback by this outburst and concerned
about the disruption of her tight schedule because she felt she
should hear more about this. Was this a whining, dependent
woman who drove her spouse away, or was he still behaving like a
bachelor who preferred his pals to "mama" but appreciated the
comforts provided? The physician quickly decided that she or
somebody should see the couple and proceed from there.

The term "midlife crisis," which occurred to her, has become a
label that gets applied to almost any form of unhappiness, misfor-
tune or psychosocial stress of people in their 30s, 40s and 50s. The
vignette could be an example of midlife crisis, but suggested
unresolved tasks in marriage and family life antedating midlife. Mr.
G might also be concerned about his parents' health and not just
be overattached to them.

We should note that we are considering "midlife" as the middle of adulthood, not the midpoint of the chronological lifespan.

Risks

When professional ambitions or economic expectations are disproportionate to parental abilities or education, or when expectations for school performance are out of line with a child's intellectual endowment, the risk for continued or progressive personal and familial maladjustment becomes high. Individually the risk most likely involves depression. However, mutual recrimination, scapegoating and focusing on one issue are common forms of displacing emotional and psychosocial deficits.

Occupationally or professionally, one parent or both should have found their niche, not necessarily having realized their ambitions but feeling that they are on their way to doing so or that they are in an occupation which will suit them indefinitely. If only the husband works outside the home, he may be the first to experience a midlife crisis. It may be brought about by a gradual or sudden sense of discrepancy between his hopes and ambitions and the reality of his accomplishments. He may compare himself with his peers. Awareness that his body is no longer as athletic or his sexual performance as vigorous as formerly may disturb him. His moods may rapidly change, or he may upset his wife with impulsive and for him unusual decisions. He may increasingly resort to alcohol, especially when there is a family history of alcoholism or if friends and peers rely on alcohol to establish a social atmosphere. This often occurs in the form of "having a beer with the boys" after work or of having multiple martini lunches.

The wife who has been mainly occupied with home and children may also experience a crisis when the house becomes empty. Some women feel "left out" and frustrated when they see their husbands enjoy the excitement and the prestige of a job or profession, or when the children become involved with their own friends, as they should. Some women feel isolated, bored, stagnant as they become disillusioned by the routine of marital life. Women whose lives are focused mainly on the activities of their children are at risk for an early "empty nest" syndrome. They react to the growing independence and separation of their children from the family with a depression. At this stage of the life cycle, women ought to explore new extrafamilial activities or interests such as employment, church activities, resumption of a career, or volunteer work.

It may be difficult for either spouse to empathize with the frustration of the marital partner. Each may complain about the other's perceived lack of support or understanding. A family's supportive social network can play an important role to prevent further deterioration. Each partner or both may receive support from recreational, social, religious or other interest groups and avoid the sense of isolation with its deleterious effects on mood and self-esteem. Women at home who lack the connections and the stimulation available at a workplace need a sustaining and even a growth-promoting social support system. Access to formal counseling with clergy or other community worker is often facilitated through friends.

A couple who have failed to form a true marital and parental coalition, as suggested by the vignette, must now be helped to catch up. If they can work and succeed belatedly in forming a coalition, they will function as a couple and not as two individuals still in a quasi-dating relationship, with each having primary interest in peers rather than each other. Continued coalition failure, especially after parenthood has occurred, will aggravate marital unhappiness, leading often to separation, with divorce a likely outcome without marital or individual counseling.

The absence of a parental coalition often sets the stage for close dyads between a parent and one of the children, which involve inappropriate psychological and even physical intimacy, a transgression of the generational boundary. This situation, usually rooted in difficulties with intimacy, may not be corrected even in a second marriage, where the same pattern may repeat itself. Professional help to prevent such repetition is often necessary.

Divorce may not always be the worst outcome. For example, one partner, having outgrown the other in various ways, may be prepared and able to undertake a more mature and harmonious relationship in the future. The first step might be what Mrs. G did—complain to an outsider about the problem. Then, if the couple were seen together, the physician or counselor might discover that the partner is also unhappy and that the couple might work out a satisfactory and more mature relationship between themselves. Divorce, though remedial for particular situations, is seldom a completely constructive event for all family members and, therefore, should initially be considered a risk condition for all involved. Marriages get dissolved, but families live on, fragmented or not. Parenthood can terminate through death, but even then mental images have been absorbed and incorporated in children's personalities. The marriage, good or bad, intact or splintered, continues to affect all family members.

Preventive Interventions

An important consideration in viewing a family with parents in midlife is to speculate how the family will cope with their children's emancipation. Are the parents as a couple sufficiently close and resilient to master their children's strivings toward independence? These strivings are at times aggressive and divisive, and may present challenges to parental values. Thus, intervention at the stage indicated in the vignette can also be viewed as a way to prevent familial and personal disruptions when the children progress to their adolescence and beyond.

In middle life, when the reproductive family phase may have ended either by choice or through the climacteric, tangible social life change decisions need to be made. If one parent has been primarily occupied with childcare and nurturing, this is the time to look after his or her peer relationships, possibly assuming work outside the home or resuming an interrupted career. Other risks at this stage may be identified as inadequate communication among family members, such as some inappropriate need for secretiveness, possibly about serious misbehavior such as substance abuse by any member, or masking conflicts instead of mastering them, or undue intrusiveness toward children, or disrespect for their individuality. These risks may evolve into serious impediments in adolescence, and such aberrations are common findings in the background of schizophrenics.

Preventive measures begin with identifying the nature of the "secret" or other reasons for reticence. Then appropriate referral to a youth or drug program or one of the "Anonymous" groups for parents can be implemented. In personal terms, as already indicated, this is the period of life when people need to feel that their life situation—familial and social—is satisfactory or is moving toward a satisfactory stage. Another connotation of the phrase "middle age" or "midlife" concerns the fact that such people are also in the middle between two generations—their children and their aging parents. If the latter are healthy and happy, wholesome and enjoyable three-generational systems can exist. In midlife one is likely to be obligated to deal with adolescent, possibly rebellious children, or "children" who, although adult, are still dependent due to unfinished education, as well as grandparents who may have retired but may need emotional or tangible support because of economic or health vicissitudes or both. This "middle squeeze" can be stressful economically, psychologically and socially. All three generations may experience stresses which, if not monitored and mastered, become a risk for depression and other psychopathology.

Menopause may be a risk condition for women and, therefore, for marriages and families, although its role remains uncertain. Middle-aged women have a lifetime prevalence of depression of 24% (Weissman & Myers, 1978), indicating many factors other than "the change of life." Aside from the discomforts engendered by the endocrine shifts, middle-aged women face significant role changes, especially if they have been full-time housewives/mothers for two or three decades. It remains to be seen if the increasing involvement of women in the work force outside the home will alter this risk for depression. So far the evidence indicates that widowed or divorced women carry the highest risk for depression or other illnesses, but for married women, a profession or work outside the home reduces the risk for depression, although their continuing familial role remains important. A close, confiding relationship with a spouse or friend appears to be a major factor in diminishing the risk for depression, otherwise some form of preventive counseling is in order.

If the wife joins the work force, it may change the equilibrium in the marriage. Not only children but husbands may feel deprived by the wife's regular absence. Also some men may resent their wives working. In either instance, marital conflict and instability may ensue and affect their leadership functions adversely. Such conflicts may be displaced by focusing on a child's difficulties, which may, in turn, be his or her reaction to the parental absences and tension. A further risk can follow if a child's problems seem to unite parents in their concern, thus keeping their basic conflict hidden from them—a situation which can also provide an impetus for perpetuating the child's symptoms. If help is sought, these issues need to be considered and resolved, possibly through a family consultation. Teachers, clergy or friends—the first to notice symptoms—may be approached by some family members.

Lastly, if the mother does double duty in a full-time job outside the home and in one equally demanding at home without increased support from the husband, the risk of overwork and exhaustion arises. Marital counseling may be indicated to alleviate this problem.

The physician and her staff evaluated the G family in terms of the five parameters of family functioning. It was difficult to determine the leader in this family. Mr. G clearly left the decisions about the children and some aspects of the home to his wife, yet he hung on to leadership in the area of finance and major purchases, with the advice of his mother. The leadership seemed divided into traditional roles, but rested also partly outside the nuclear family.

The boundaries between the generations seemed to be clearly drawn in this traditional family. However, since the relationship between Mr. and Mrs. G had grown distant, Mrs. G had turned to the children for closeness and emotional support. In meeting her own needs, Mrs. G had blurred the parent-child boundaries.

There was a notable absence of intimacy between the spouses. Mrs. G had kept her feelings to herself about her husband's withdrawal and his attachment to his family of origin. These feelings were not easily talked about or shared on either side. Their respective resentments remained underground, but affected the family's emotional climate adversely.

Communication was similarly lacking in the G family. It was as if there were a tacit agreement not to talk about the central issue dividing husband and wife. The anger and jealousy came out, however, in petty arguments and bickering, which created a negative climate of tension.

Ideally families function at this stage in close harmony. A salubrious emotional climate conducive to the growth of the children has been established, and the spouses, after perhaps giving up some of their earlier dreams, have found their niche. This climate was not present in the G family, setting the stage for a midlife crisis, perhaps primarily affecting Mrs. G, who felt isolated and bored as her earlier ideals of marriage had not been realized.

This family is at risk for divorce and its consequences. Whether divorce occurs or not, without change this family will remain "fatherless" with an inadequate male role model, not necessarily because the father is inadequate but because his spouse presents him thus. This can then lead to repetition of the pattern by a son in his own future functioning as a father or by a daughter in her selection of a mate. Children can also "act out" in a "fatherless" family to test whether a father cares enough about them to set limits.

After listening to Mrs. G's tearful story, the doctor asked the nurse to spend more time with Mrs. G to gather more data. It seemed to them that Mrs. G had never really communicated her frustration to Mr. G about his withdrawal to his own family because she feared his anger, perhaps his walking out on her, as had happened in her own parents' marriage. The doctor and nurse decided to support Mrs. G in opening up the subject to Mr. G, but were also concerned that a release of her stored-up anger "out of the blue" might serve to drive her husband further away. The couple needed to recapture some of their closeness of earlier years. Mrs. G was encouraged to plan a time together for them to be alone and enjoy a special activity that could bring back warm memories. If Mrs. G could initiate a dialogue about the deterioration of their relationship, perhaps Mr. G could be convinced to seek couple counseling to work out their problem together. The practitioner could then be in a position to make a referral for specialized help in a marital or family agency if necessary.

This plan worked out very well. Mrs. G arranged for a dinner out on their anniversary when she could point out how their marriage had changed and that they needed help to get it back on track. Mr. G was quite agreeable to this proposal and let her know that he too did not like their increasing separateness.

In summary, the early midlife family can constitute the most fulfilling phase of the family cycle, but as indicated by the vignette, it is also a period when risks can be identified through complaints as presented by Mrs. G and preventive intervention brought about.

LATE MIDDLE LIFE

> Mrs. K, age 56, had looked forward to her husband's retirement, but it was not working out as she had anticipated. It seemed as if she had just "gotten rid of the last one" when their oldest daughter with a child came back to stay with her parents after separation from her husband. Mr. and Mrs. K had thought they could get along on his retirement income, but that was now insufficient and he was pressing Mrs. K to return to light assembly factory work, which she had left many years ago to have their children. She did not think she could do this now because of her physical problems—back aches, swollen ankles and chest pain—for which she increasingly saw her doctor. No physical cause could be found for these complaints. She claimed she could not stand the "stress" of work again.

Late midlife, the sixth and seventh decades of life, can be a period when people feel settled in their lives, when tangible family tasks are mostly completed, when grandparenthood can be welcomed and enjoyed, provided that people are basically healthy and satisfied with or reconciled to their psychosocial existence.

Late midlife parents are now also at an age when the death of their own parents is increasingly likely, even imminent. This contingency can bring home their own mortality with surprising force, producing in some a reassessment of their place in life, and with others the risk of depression.

Death of any member affects the survivors not only from the health standpoint, but also because for the aging it may precipitate social isolation. The loss of a middle-aged son or daughter is becoming relatively more common as more and more people survive beyond the seventh or eighth decade. Mourning as a trigenerational family is necessarily a function of prior familial relationships. If they were poor, they become at this stage of late middle age a source of problems as well as risks for disease.

Coping effectively with separation is important at every phase of the life cycle. But at this stage, it is critical because losses are apt to occur as parents' parents may die and children leave home.

If life as a couple is to be resumed, a new marital adjustment needs to be achieved, which as noted before can be either welcome or very difficult. After retirement(s) the couple may have to learn how to spend entire days together. In trigenerational or extended family systems, the rights and needs of all adults must be respected.

Risks

Declining physical and sexual powers can produce marital stress, especially if the partners have not found new ways to enjoy each other as coparents or as sexual partners. Marital disharmony and emotional distress such as depression or the so-called empty nest syndrome are frequent complications of this life phase.

Other risks to mental health arise from the more frequent occurrence of physical ailments such as degenerative diseases, malignancies, and organic brain syndromes. Some of these unfortunately are not preventable unless they are secondary to treatable conditions such as hypertension or myxedema. Physicians must be aware that patients with depressions often present themselves with physical complaints. Furthermore, some depressions may simulate organic brain syndromes if patients experience difficulty in concentrating, which may lead to forgetfulness, inattention and the claim, if not the fact, that they cannot do many things that they used to do routinely. In such instances, it is too late for preventive measures, but appropriate, prompt and adequate treatment of the underlying depression can reverse these "deficits." Furthermore, a woman like Mrs. K might benefit from joining some activity group through a church or a community agency.

Although separation and divorce as such are not clinical issues, at times health professionals are sought for consultation prior to, during and after divorce. The risks for ill health after separation and divorce are considerable, as they are also for widowhood (Jacobs & Douglas, 1979). Mourning is a normative process, but if prolonged may become a pathological condition, and health personnel in general need to be aware that the acute mourning phase is not distinguishable from depressive illness. If recovery and reconstitution from the acute mourning stage do not occur in a period of a few months, it should be considered pathological and an indication for therapeutic intervention. Thus, some health surveillance and follow-up for the bereaved, whether divorced or widowed, are always indicated.

The vignette indicates one type of risk for depression in the form of physical complaints rooted in prolonged parenthood when welcome relief from parental chores was expected. In general, children's failure to achieve a level of adulthood wished for by parents or expected by the society in which they live is one common source of conflict and unwanted burden for people in middle age, the more so if they also still carry responsibilities for their own aging and possibly infirm parents. Risks for maladjustments and ill health are enhanced if one or both breadwinners are retired at this point, which is the more likely the less skilled the primary breadwinner was at his or her final level of employment. A retirement income may be adequate for a couple, but insufficient for the additional support of parents or children. However, a single or divorced daughter with dependent children on welfare may supplement the household income. Trigenerational households may have fiscal advantages but also pose risks for the emotional health of the family, and may interfere with the personal and emotional growth of the young parent.

Another risk for this age group arises from the necessity or decision to change domiciles. Such moves may entail disadvantages not always foreseen by the middle-aged person or couple, such as more severe separation reactions than anticipated upon leaving familiar surroundings, relatives or friends. This risk exists whether the move is a voluntary one to the Sunbelt, or a necessary one to a communal setting from an independent home dictated by economic conditions or ill health. Such relocations may lead to more social isolation than expected; couples may have to live "more intimately" in close quarters than they find comfortable, in addition to being in unfamiliar surroundings.

Preventive Interventions

Education about midlife family issues ought to be available but is hard to come by unless there is a knowledgeable physician or other health worker, clergy or other adviser, even a wise friend, around. Mothers whose tangible parental tasks have ended may need help to find suitable work, reinvolvement in education, or a social life with peers. Church groups, charitable services, or recreational organizations should make themselves known in a community and solicit middle-aged and elderly people, whether retired from mothering or jobs.

All frontline practitioners should be aware of and help spouses recognize and adjust to the empty nest or to the reduced tasks in the not-quite-empty nest, thereby reducing or eliminating risks for further maladjustments.

Lastly, parents in the "middle squeeze" should have access to family services to procure assistance and support as needed, lest they become overburdened. Intervention may entail advice and information about available services such as meals on wheels, day-care for the aged, transportation for the infirm, and so forth. It is important to make the availability of services known to this age group, and frontline personnel therefore must be alert and sensitive in discerning such needs, even if the advisee or patient does not or cannot make them explicit.

Leadership in a trigenerational household is usually diffuse, unless there is a firm cultural tradition that the eldest person is the boss. Intergenerational boundaries are also blurred with two generations of adults. Emotionally and cognitively, children may benefit from the opportunity to interact and communicate with several adults of different ages. This opportunity is often marred if conflicts prevail, familial roles are unclear, or all feel unduly burdened by their life tasks, as did Mrs. K.

Mrs. K's problem was depression, although no depressive symptoms as such were presented by her. She might well have been given antidepressant medication, but resolution of the familial dilemma would be indicated to prevent further health deterioration, with or without depression. Minimally, a consultation with the family as a group was indicated and possibly continued family therapy to explore satisfactory and constructive resolution of the psychological, social and economic issues.

The physician referred Mrs. K to a family agency, recommending that all members be seen as a group. The social worker established that the daughter and child were eligible for public support, and eventually induced the daughter to prepare herself for work through vocational rehabilitation. Daycare for the baby was arranged so that Mrs. K did not have to function as a full-time babysitter. The trigenerational household was preserved and a goal agreed upon. The daughter would establish herself independently once she could support herself, and Mrs. K would remain available as a babysitter for periods when the child could not be in daycare or nursery school. Mr. K agreed to continue working until the daughter could leave. Mrs. K recovered without antidepressant medication.

REFERENCES

Greenspan, S.I., & Pollack, G.H. (Eds.) (1980). *The course of life. Vol. 3. Adulthood and aging process.* DHHS Publ. No. (ADM) 80. Washington, DC: US Government Printing Office.

Jacobs, S., & Douglas, L. (1979). Grief: A mediating process between a loss and illness. *Comprehensive Psychiatry, 20,* 165–176.

Kasl, S.F., Gore, S., & Cobb, S. (1975). The experience of losing a job: Reported changes in health, symptoms and illness behavior. *Psychosomatic Medicine, 37,* 106.

Levinson, D.J. (1978). *The seasons of a man's life.* New York: Knopf.

Neugarten, B.L. (1964). *Personality in middle life and late life.* New York: Atherton.

Parkes, C.M., & Weiss, R.S. (1983). *Recovery from bereavement.* New York: Basic Books.

Smith, G.R., Jr., Monson, R.A., & Ray, D.C. (1986). Psychiatric consultation in somatization disorders. *New England Journal of Medicine, 314,* 1407–1413.

Weissman, M.M., & Myers, J.K. (1978). Affective disorders in a U.S. urban community. *Archives of General Psychiatry, 35,* 1304–1311.

Weissman, M.M., Paykel, E., & Klerman, G. (1972). The depressed woman as a mother. *Social Psychiatry, 7,* 98–108.

11
AGING

Mrs. E, aged 82, had never made friends easily, but after her husband died the previous year, she went into virtual seclusion. Her friends first came around regularly, even though she did not call them, but they gradually drifted away. She found it difficult to deal with finances, but was too proud to ask her sons for assistance. She felt too embarrassed to reveal her helplessness. She found it more difficult to sleep and gradually increased her glass of wine before bedtime to three or four. She was growing more forgetful and several times awoke at night in the living room with a cigarette smoldering on the sofa and the stove left on. Neighbors called her to the attention of the lay minister who visited the elderly and households in that parish.

The minister found Mrs. E to be open and personable on the first visit but felt that Mrs. E did not remember her when she returned a week later. Mrs. E had seemed responsive to her suggestion of joining the church's senior citizens club, but had forgotten to go to the meeting. After several visits and false starts, the minister told Mrs. E that she wanted her doctor's name so that she could arrange to take her for a check-up. At the appointment, the minister told the physician that she was willing to work with Mrs. E to help her develop better coping skills and access to community resources, but that she wanted physical problems ruled out first.

The minister knew that about 5% of people over the age of 65 are affected with dementia (Greenspan & Pollock, 1980), and if this were Mrs. E's problem, she wanted a definite diagnosis and any treatment possible. Mrs. E was not acting like others in her age group and health bracket. If she was depressed, the lay minister could think of several strategies she might use to help her; but she also wanted an opinion on drug therapy. She decided to delay contacting Mrs. E's sons until after the check-up. If there were no serious medical problems, there would be time to help Mrs. E recognize the need for interdependence with family members and others, while supporting her sense of worth as a woman, parent and grandparent. The lay minister decided that if hospitalization were recommended, she would then ask Mrs. E to notify her sons.

Mrs. E presents a typical diagnostic task, the differentiation among dementia, Alzheimer's disease, arteriosclerotic brain disease, and pseudodementia due to depression. Differential diagnosis may be difficult to establish even with expert examination, and a therapeutic trial with antidepressants may be indicated. Like the examination, such a drug trial may not be conclusive. Most people with Alzheimer-type dementia will become depressed as they become aware of their progressive cognitive deficits. Such individuals often react with shame if not guilt, more so if they have previously prided themselves on their mental and social competence and independence.

All people are sometimes sad and lonely. Some aged persons suffer from depression. Some simply enjoy life. Others wax philosophical about the inexorable changes in patterns of life with the passage of time and the aging process. Yet another personality type finds compensation for growing old: retirement from work, recreation, grandchildren, travel or religion. Our "young country" now has at least as many senior citizens clubs as scout troops. Eighty percent of older people are active and live independently without major handicaps or illness well into the ninth decade (Roca et al., 1984).

Mrs. E's minister worked with many elderly parishioners—some who could join in daily bus excursions, others who were essentially homebound. She enjoyed these older persons and participated in their enjoyment of life.

Besides requiring a safe living environment, adequate diet, and proper health supervision, the elderly have three basic psychological needs; how these are met in their life situations must be assessed:

1. Family ties give the older person, as well as the younger generations, a sense of belonging. Without parents, possibly without siblings, the retired person can feel removed and retired from life—particularly so if childless. Contact with nieces, nephews, grandchildren or "adopted grandchildren" can reestablish a connection with society.

2. Whatever the extent of health problems, the older person needs to maintain control over the immediate environment. Whether this can be carried out through independent living, self-care tasks for the homebound, or is limited to decision making by a severely medically ill person, this sense of control is psychologically needed. The older adult is an adult, not a child. Intervention is often needed to increase empowerment of an adult who has been competent, but who is seen as a childlike person. Assisting elderly persons to control their daily lives as much as possible enhances the quality of life for them.

3. Anxiety is a normal response to growing dependence on others. Elderly persons experience anxiety over many issues: loss of health, loss of friends through death, loss of memory, loss of self-value. Anxiety over growing dependency can be allayed by leaving old people as much in control as is realistic. But leadership reversal between old people and their children can also be realistic and a source of relief for the aging.

Aging is not, of course, a chronological point in the life cycle, but rather an ongoing developmental process—progressing step by step, from the young old to the old old to the very old. These stages differ markedly—psychologically, socially and physically—in terms of strengths and vulnerabilities, life-stage related tasks, as well as kinds of risks and ways of helping to reduce them. In the vignette, Mrs. E should have had appropriate assistance to deal with her loss when she became a widow at 81. Such help might have reduced her risk of becoming ill and depressed.

The central fact of the aging process is that of diminishment and loss—with tremendous individual variations as to pace, degree and form. Thus, decrements affect one's energy, power and competencies, in relationships and social roles, in physical and mental abilities. In general, aging entails potential reductions and impairments in many or most spheres of one's life and person. The ways in which individuals react to these diminishings can spell the difference between psychological health and psychopathology. Is there, for instance, an adaptive acceptance of waning powers or instead a maladaptive denial of them? Are feasible and enjoyable compensations found or angrily refused? As Dylan Thomas (1946) put it, "Do not go gentle into that good night!"

The range of personal responses to getting old and older is such that they may best be highlighted by some other brief anecdotes.

Mrs. P, at age 83, struggled to continue the same heavy schedule she had maintained throughout a distinguished professional career. Although walking was now painful due to arthritis and she found herself more forgetful and making "silly mistakes," she reacted by blaming herself for failing to meet her lifelong standards of excellence. Despite mounting anxiety, she pushed herself even harder, causing even more fear of failure and lowered self-esteem. Finally a close friend and understanding colleague was able to help Mrs. P recognize realistic alternatives to the extremes of "business as usual" and total renunciation of any involvement in her fields of interest, which was by no means necessary.

Mr. B, aged 75, had few interests in life other than an almost full-time job of meeting the demands of his overdependent wife, plus the physically arduous tasks of maintaining their home and extensive grounds. Rather suddenly he suffered a heart attack and from then on faced a sedentary life, for which his prior patterns had ill prepared him. He felt useless, became morose, and started to berate his wife for her years of demands upon him, which he had actually encouraged and from which he had derived a sense of pride and manliness. He also sought solace in drinking too much, but this was now forbidden by his physician on medical grounds. His wife resented his sudden change from protectiveness to hostility, and in turn became very unsympathetic with regard to his problems.

As the strains between them escalated and Mr. B was bordering on a depression, a psychologically oriented friend became increasingly concerned and managed to intervene. He met with them together and separately to explain the unhappy feelings of each to the other. Inquiring about Mr. B's past interests, he found that his friend once enjoyed playing the piano. The friend sought to fan this spark into a flame of interest, and also took up with the wife how she might be able to help him regain this activity. She acknowledged there was a piano in their home that had not been used for many years and was advised to get it tuned. At first she declined, claiming it was useless; he was so apathetic and negative he would not play it. The friend persisted, and pointed out that even if he did not use it, the fact of her having it tuned for him could convey her wanting to be supportive of him, which he badly needed from her. Furthermore, since he was feeling increasingly hopeless about his own future, the very fact of readying the piano for his playing it when and if he felt like it was an implicit signal of optimism and hope for his improvement. This small intervention was based on knowledgeable sensitivity.

Although Mrs. P and Mr. B were totally dissimilar in almost every respect, including personality, education, ethnicity and medical status, they both showed a not infrequent reaction to age-related infirmities. Both of these people were relatively affluent and realistically able financially to meet the added expenses of their progressive medical needs without discomfort. Nevertheless, both became very anxious and preoccupied about money; each sought to economize to an extent that was not only needless but would also have diminished their security and the shrinking sources of enjoyment they had. Mrs. P had multiple physical handicaps and objectively needed financial reserves; her business manager assured the friend that these were ample. Mr. B, too, was about to economize by dismissing the loyal handyman who had been with the couple for years and on whose help he and his wife now fully depended. In both instances, the friends and professionals involved with these aging people were able to prevent these self-defeating and dangerous reactions by understanding that the individuals felt an impoverishment of self in terms of their age-related reduced capacities, and displaced this to a sense of financial impoverishment, which for them was actually not a reality.

RISKS

Isolation, so much a part of urban American society, is an important risk for the elderly. Widowhood in particular increases risks for physical and mental disorders. The isolated nuclear family often is not in a position to include aging parents or grandparents. Ageism, a negative attitude toward old people characteristic in particular in the United States, is another important risk source for the elderly. The customary equation of aging with illness or infirmity must be unlearned by many people, health professionals included. Aging is accompanied by declining energy and strength, but it is not a pathological process or necessarily accompanied by declining mental faculties. In the not-so-distant past, only the healthiest persons reached the ninth and tenth decades. Modern medicine has changed this and will continue to do so. Illness is more common in the aged, but not mental illness in particular, unless organic brain disease develops. However, the psychological and emotional implications of invalidism constitute important risks for depression.

Two consequences of impaired faculties, whether from depression or organicity, are demoralization and decrements in self-care. These in turn may exacerbate depression. Forgetfulness for any reason may lead to inadequate diet, danger of fire, and other security risks. If no relatives or friends are available for support and companionship, institutional care in a home for the aged or nursing facility may be indicated for adequate care, safety and supervision. Persons suffering degenerative brain disease may also eventually require institutional care.

The families of such old persons with serious medical problems also need support, care and consultative services. Relatives are usually concerned, but may take on more of the care burden than is appropriate for their health or may divert too much time and energy from their primary family tasks. Siblings and children of demented people suffer. They are losing a significant person who becomes a stranger, a child instead of a revered parent or peer. Mourning begins long before death in such instances, and preventive support and care are indicated.

The elderly person's life space shrinks when a move from a house to a small apartment or even a single room becomes necessary. While it may be something of a relief to own fewer things that need to be taken care of, new and unfamiliar surroundings can also be a source of discomfort and confusion. The loss of friends or neighbors or some personal disability may further aggravate the isolation of the elderly person.

PREVENTIVE INTERVENTIONS

Attention must be paid to such mundane matters as safety and simplicity of an aged person's surroundings, adequate lighting—including night lights—safe access and exits to and from living quarters, and provision for essential shopping. In some areas, fear of crime is realistic and further curtails an old person's mobility.

Clergy or church member, pharmacists, activity directors, social workers, directors of volunteers, and health care providers are all in a position to spot developing problems. Helping elderly people to accept dependence for whatever reason is an important task for service providers. Such acceptance can become critical for those persons who have always prided themselves on their mental and social competence and personal independence. Mrs. E, for instance, will need "permission" and encouragement in learning to depend upon her sons and others. Learning about appropriate agencies, hot lines, emergency services, Meals on Wheels, and recreational facilities available to the elderly can enhance their lives, especially for those who are isolated and live alone.

An "exchange" between generations can be of mutual benefit. Thus, for instance, older naturalized Americans may teach their native tongues to students in return for companionship and transportation. Senior citizens clubs providing social, emotional, mental and recreational opportunities are becoming increasingly accepted. Activities reduce the sense of helplessness and the apprehension of becoming increasingly dependent on others. Foster grandparents can renew their sense of self-worth by nurturing, teaching and offering help to young children. A pet provides companionship and bolsters self-esteem by making a person feel needed.

Barriers to comprehensive care include ageism, poverty, disengaged families, unenlightened health care workers, and lack of affordable homes or nursing homes for the aged, as well as concern about "intruding" into others' lives. Sometimes preventive or treatment measures are fragmented: The right medication is prescribed but its cost proves prohibitive; referrral to an appropriate agency occurs but transportation is unavailable; grown children want to be involved but feel guilty "telling" an aged parent what to do. Proper care of the elderly requires consideration of their daily needs and preventive and therapeutic interventions on many levels.

Fear of death and of dying are important risks for ill health; therefore, caretakers of older people need to face and tactfully discuss this inevitable eventuality with their clients. Hospices were instituted first in England by Dr. Cicely Saunders in the 1950s for the care of dying patients and bereaved families. The hospice movement, which includes in- and outpatient care, is gaining ground in this country, although as yet too slowly to meet the need. In such settings of understanding care—medical and psychological— the losses of dignity and sense of personal worth for people at death's door have been greatly reduced (Zack, 1979).

Mrs. E's physician screened her for organic illness and then decided on a therapeutic trial of antidepressants, explaining to the minister that at least until the next appointment Mrs. E was not to self-administer the medication. It was arranged that volunteers from the parish would step in to visit Mrs. E each evening. They usually brought her a snack in addition to supervising her taking her antidepressant. A month later, the physician was delighted to hear from both the minister and Mrs. E that she had attended a senior citizens meeting and signed up for a day trip to the casinos. She showed no evidence of mania, just more energy and interest in life. As Mrs. E began to feel more in control of her life, she was given charge of her medication. Only very slowly did she begin to call upon her sons to help her with major decisions, financial arrangements, and eventually with moving out of the family home. On the second anniversary of her husband's death, she invited some of her friends for dinner, and among other things they talked about the loneliness of widowhood.

The minister had a multitude of resources available: a competent physician, concerned neighbors and parishioners, reliable relatives, and an active senior citizens club. Mrs. E was a person at risk because she was isolated and because she felt her coping skills declining, which in turn demoralized her. The minister knew how to mobilize the resources, and fortunately Mrs. E's condition was reversible. She could be helped and restored to much better functioning with the help of antidepressant medication and mobilized social supports.

> Mr. S, aged 75, suffered pain due to lung cancer and was no longer strong enough to be self-sufficient, which had been a source of pride for him prior to his illness. He was demoralized by his helpless dependence and terminal condition, and his distress was intensified by his realization that Roberta, his youngest daughter, seemed to resent having had to bear, over several years, the main burden of his care. His home, where he had remained with Roberta since his illness began, was no haven of warmth and affection—it had become a bitter battleground for family strife. His other children became more aware of old schisms and rivalry among them when it became time to appoint a conservator and they discovered that their father had never written a will. When some of Roberta's siblings showed an increased interest in their father, she became suspicious that they were now more interested in the money than in his welfare. Two of her siblings, however, distanced themselves and did not want to have anything to do with the "whole mess."

For Mr. S there were still opportunities to reduce his despair and to help restore his sense of dignity and intactness as a person. His physician referred him to a nurse of the hospice home care program.

The nurse learned of the patient's failure to make a will, which might reflect the patient's fear and self-defeating denial of his impending death. Facing one's mortality and preparing a will and directions for one's end and disposal are mental health issues that can fester or can be dealt with in a helpful and reassuring manner. Earlier help might also have forestalled or reduced the emotionally destructive family quarrels. The nurse succeeded in restoring to Mr. S some power to control his own destiny. As is common, he feared the process of dying more than death itself; he dreaded an enforced prolongation by "heroic" measures of dying in an impersonal, lonely hospital setting. He worried that he might become too incapacitated to express his refusal of such treatment or that his refusal might be ignored. The nurse could relieve his fear by helping him to execute a living will with the support of his physician and conservator. This action proved an antidote to a major source of his anxiety. Living wills have become legalized in a majority of states. Even where this is not so, they carry increased influence with courts and hospitals.

The vignette illustrates how the impending death of a family member often activates latent family conflicts and sibling rivalries. At this point little family-focused prevention could be initiated. However, the younger generation might well be advised to seek some consultation with a mental health professional, especially after Mr. S's death, so that his grandchildren and their parents might be spared similar family conflicts.

> Ninety-two-year-old Miss T lived alone in her family home after her three sisters died. Her cognitive functioning was good but other health problems abounded: impaired hearing and eyesight, and poor mobility due to osteoporosis and osteoarthritis and circulatory insufficiency. Her hygiene and disposition were poor.
>
> Miss T's family consisted of two middle-aged distant cousins who lived nearby and their respective families. Both cousins stopped in weekly for 30-minute visits, but both dreaded these visits. They saw the swollen arms, black eyes, and bruised legs from Miss T's falls. They heard that she had

fired Meals on Wheels, which they had arranged. Miss T did not like "that girl" who was employed to come in three half-days a week to do housekeeping and grocery shopping. The cousins took turns transporting Miss T to clinic appointments and delivering holiday meals to her home. On occasion they risked Miss T's ridicule and rage by suggesting a retirement community or nursing home. Nobody wanted Miss T to join them for the holidays and there was no possibility of her living with either family.

Serious concern existed because of Miss T's decision to leave her back door unlocked because she was too deaf to hear the doorbell and because of her poor nutrition, as she ate mostly pastries after firing Meals on Wheels. Despite her tendency to fall, she insisted that she could take care of herself, did not want a medical alarm system, did not intend to share her home, and would not give it up to "live in a nut house."

Like so many elderly persons, Miss T retained as many strengths as she had disabilities. Her mental alertness, independence, pride and stubbornness were lifelong characteristics. For 35 years she had taught school and was accustomed to being treated with respect and dignity. She was all too close to the truth in her disparagement of nursing homes when she predicted, "The first thing they do is not like the way I stay up late at night and the way I insist on what I want and deserve. They would have their doctor give me sedatives so that I wouldn't bother them."

Her family physician of many decades, with whom she had had a trusting relationship, had retired some years before and referred her to an HMO to ensure that some physician would always be on call for her. Although she had a primary physician there, he had seen her only a few times for rather routine problems and prescriptions, and no close relationship had developed. Unfortunately, each time she asked for a home visit, a different physician came and she got too annoyed—"tired"—at having to repeat her medical history.

A preventive opportunity was missed here, probably because her former physician underrated or ignored his importance to his patient. He might have considered a referral for Miss T to a colleague who could and would relate to her and not make her feel devalued as "just a number" in a clinic. Also the primary HMO physician might have made a routine house call to see firsthand how this woman lived and possibly sought advice of a social worker or mental health worker.

Allowing aged persons to use the range of their capabilities and to respect their need for the familiar can prevent health problems or at least complications. Proper assistance and safeguards may enable them to avoid nursing home care, which many elderly rightly view as an assault on their dignity and sense of self.

Yet the risks indicated in the vignette were real, although a mental health problem per se had not arisen. Miss T's emotional state had remained constant throughout her adulthood. She had a sharp mind, sharp opinions, and a sharp tongue. Her insistence on remaining in her own home was reasonable. The problem as seen by her cousins was one of physical safety.

An important resource in this case was her carefully accrued life savings and the ownership of a second house. However, like many elderly people she refused to spend any of her savings or even the rent she received from the second house. The cousins feared correctly that the situation could only change following an injury such as a fractured hip when Miss T was home alone and unable to obtain emergency help. She would then be forced to accept institutional care.

Fortunately, one of the cousin's grown children, a social worker married to a nurse, brought about a solution. They lived in a different state, visited Miss T only a few times a year, and were not embroiled in the struggle over her independence. After one visit, they wrote Miss T a detailed letter. They told her they admired her independence and stamina and agreed with her decision to live in her own home. They then very clearly outlined what she had to do and what she had to spend to make her home safe. Specific changes were: 1) Hire a woman to come in the late afternoon, prepare supper, do dishes and arrange a cold breakfast in the refrigerator. They suggested that this worker read or watch television in a separate room and not encroach on Miss T's space during the evening. At 11:00 p.m. the employee would lock up the house and go home. 2) An emergency alarm system was to be installed that would alert an ambulance in case of a fall. 3) The woman who cleaned and bought groceries should continue to be employed three half-days a week.

After receiving this letter, Miss T showed it to her cousins in a manner that suggested "Why weren't you clever enough to think of this?" The middle-aged women chose to overlook the tone, and instead began immediately to arrange the interviews for the evening worker and to have the alarm system installed. This arrangement allowed Miss T to live in her home for another four years.

From a systems viewpoint, there was, of course, no family left here, and Miss T had been her own "leader" for over seven decades. Her boundaries had shrunk, but what was inside was critically important to her. She did not feel loved by anybody who failed to respect her willfulness and independence, which left the concerned cousins "out in the cold." Communication with them, therefore, was unproductive and cantankerous. The task of providing Miss T with the help for her physical disabilities and ensuring her safety could be accomplished only after she felt reassured that her fierce need for independence was appreciated and taken into account.

REFERENCES

Berlin, R.M., & Sluzki, C.E. (1987). C-L psychiatry and the family system. *Psychosomatics, 28,* 206–208.

Bok, S. (1976). Personal directions for care at the end of life. *New England Journal of Medicine, 295,* 367–369.

Brody, S., Poulshock, S., & Masciocchi, C. (1978). The family caring unit: A major consideration in the long-term support system. *Gerontology, 18,* 556–560.

Dunlop, B.D. (1980). Expanded home-based care for the impaired elderly: Solution or pipe dream? *American Journal of Public Health, 70,* 514–519.

Erickson, E.H., Erickson, T.M., & Kivnick, H.I. (1986). *Vital involvement in old age.* New York: W.W. Norton.

Gaza, A. (1986). Living wills. *Manhattan Medicine, 5,* 15.

Greenspan, S.I., & Pollock, G.H. (1980). *The course of life. Vol. 3. Adulthood and aging process.* DHHS Pub. No. (ADM) 80. Washington, DC: US Government Printing Office.

Griffith, J.L., & Griffith, M.E. (1987). Structural family therapy in chronic illness. *Psychosomatics, 28,* 202–205.

Hay, J.W., & Ernst, R.L. (1987). The economic cost of Alzheimer's disease. *American Journal of Public Health, 77,* 1169–1175.

Helsing, K.J., & Szklo, M. (1981). Mortality after bereavement. *American Journal of Epidemiology, 114,* 41–52.

Keith, P.M. (1986). Isolation of the unmarried in later life. *Family Relations, 35,* 389–395.

Lieberman, P.B., & Jacobs, S.C. (1987). Bereavement and its complications in medical patients: A guide for consultation-liaison psychiatrists. *International Journal of Psychiatry in Medicine, 17,* 23–39.

Lindemann, E. (1944). Symptomatology and management of acute grief. *American Journal of Psychiatry, 101,* 141–148.

Roca, R.P., Klein, L.E., Kirby, S.M., et al. (1984). Recognition of dementia among medical patients. *Archives of Internal Medicine, 144,* 73–75.

Rowe, J.W., & Kahn, R.L. (1987). Human aging: Usual and successful. *Science, 237,* 143–149.

Society for the Right to Die. (1987). Handbook of living will laws. New York: Author.

Somers, A.R. (1987). Insurance for long-term care. *New England Journal of Medicine, 317,* 23–29.

Thomas, D. (1946). *The collected poems.* New York: James Laughlin.

Zack, S. (1979). Hospice—A concept of care in the final stages of life. *Connecticut Medicine, 43,* 367–372.

12

CONCLUDING COMMENTS

It is usually difficult to validate the old proverb that an ounce of prevention is worth a pound of cure and demonstrate this truth, especially in the mental health field. Even the premise that it is worthwhile to improve the quality of life for the general population and for families and children in particular is not popular, although the disadvantages of poverty, of inadequate housing, of inferior schools, and of disorganized neighborhoods are well known.

In this report, we focus primarily on the family as a unit and its growth- and health-promoting functions through the family life cycle. Viewing the family as a system, however, also includes possible innate weaknesses or defects in the child as well as in the community's impact on family functioning.

We identify risk factors in children and their environments, which, if they could be eliminated or reduced, could result in a significant decrease in the incidence and prevalence of some of the common childhood mental and emotional disorders. It is possible to intervene at any point in the life cycle. Focus for intervention can be on the individual at different stages of development, on the family in its different life cycle phases, on the family at times of crisis, on the subcultural environment in which the family lives, on the institutions and agencies that have impact on the developing individual, and on the sociopolitical matrix. Intervention at any one of these levels may alter personal and environmental conditions and facilitate more competent functioning of all individuals involved and of the family as a unit.

Sociopolitical action and advocacy by professionals are necessary. Children have no vote, and, as Jefferson asserted, only an informed electorate can make democracy work. Informing the electorate about health matters, mental health in particular, is our task as professionals, as is advocacy for providing optimal conditions for every child to grow into an adult who is as healthy as possible and can pursue life fully, limited only by possible inborn or acquired handicaps.

The concepts outlined in this report of possible maldevelopment throughout the life cycle are not new for the most part. They have been largely ignored, however, and in particular have not been used for the identification of risks to mental health. Our emphasis on the family as a possibly malfunctioning system, and how to evaluate this system of which the child is only one element, is a new approach.

Appropriate preparation and readiness for parenthood, an awareness of the life cycle changes outlined in this report, and the capacity to master these transitions are essential for personal and familial health and welfare. Shortcomings in these respects constitute risks to mental health.

This report is directed to parents, teachers, frontline health personnel, and other caregivers to enable them to identify developmental lags, family imbalances, and other signals of risk and assist them in their efforts to initiate risk-reducing measures. We have tried to describe and illustrate by case examples how people need to learn to cope with changes in their lives as they pass through the life cycle and how they can be assisted in mastering these transitions.

Although the effectiveness of many risk-reducing measures has been demonstrated, it remains a controversial issue. The value of public policies favoring preventive interventions has been questioned again and again when investments of money and efforts were compared to possible benefits, because these are as elusive as any concept of health. Thus interventions in terms of the greatest good to the largest percentage of the population are still hotly debated. However, a family without identifiable risk or pathology is healthier than one in which risk factors are found.

Furthermore, our citizenry, and therefore our government(s), have failed to acknowledge and remedy the grossly adverse conditions for health and mental health attached to poverty, often associated with single parenthood, parental unemployability due to inadequate or interrupted schooling, lack of toys and books, disinterest in reading, and a pervading sense of powerlessness. Such conditions are serious threats—risks—for optimal personal development and for family unity and functioning. To repeat, much of what is contained in this report is not new but awaits implementation of what was advocated by the first White House Conference on Children almost 60 years ago in the Child's Bill of Rights.

THE CHILD'S BILL OF RIGHTS

The ideal to which we should strive is that there shall be no child in America:

That has not been born under proper conditions

That does not live in hygienic surroundings

That ever suffers from undernourishment

That does not have prompt and efficient medical attention and inspection

That does not receive primary instruction in the elements of hygiene and good health

That has not the complete birthright of a sound mind in a sound body

That has not the encouragement to express in fullest measure the spirit within which is the final endowment of every human being.

Herbert Hoover

BIBLIOGRAPHY

Ackerknecht, E.H. (1954). *Rudolf Virchow, doctor, statesman, anthropologist.* Madison, WI: Wisconsin University Press.

Ackerman, N.W. (1958). *The psychodynamics of family life.* New York: Basic Books.

Adams, B.N. (1975). *The American family: A sociological interpretation.* Chicago: Rand McNally.

Aldrich, C.K. (1975). Office psychotherapy for the primary care physician. In D.X. Freedman & Jarl E. Dyrud (Eds.), *American handbook of psychiatry* (Vol. 5, 2nd ed.). New York: Basic Books.

Anthony, E.J., & Koupernick, C. (Eds.) (1974). *The child in his family: Children at psychiatric risk* (Vol. 3). New York: Wiley.

Anthony, E.J., Koupernick, C., & Chiland, C. (Eds.) (1978). *The child in his family: Vulnerable children* (Vol. 4). New York: Wiley.

Aries, P. (1965). *Centuries of childhood.* New York: Vintage Books.

Barter, J.T., & Talbott, S.W. (Eds.) (1986). *Primary prevention.* Washington, DC: American Psychiatric Press.

Bernay, T., & Cantor, D. (1986). *The psychology of today's women.* Hillsdale, NJ: Analytic Press.

Bertalanffy, L. von (1986). *Organismic psychology and systems theory.* Worcester, MA: Clark University Press.

Blaker, R.M. (1980). *Studies of familial communication and psychopathology.* Oslo: Universitetsforlaget.

Bloom, M. (1981). *Primary prevention: The possible science.* New York: Prentice-Hall.

Bowlby, J. (1969, 1973, 1980). *Attachment and loss* (Vol. 1); *Separation, anxiety and anger* (Vol. 2); *Loss, sadness and depression* (Vol. 3). New York: Basic Books.

Brazelton, T.B. (1981). *On becoming a family. The growth of attachment.* New York: Delacort/Seymour Lawrence.

Butler, R.N., & Lewis, M.I. (1977). *Aging and mental health: Positive psychosocial approaches.* St. Louis: C.V. Mosby.

Cath, S.H., Gurwitt, A.R., & Ross, J.M. (Eds.) (1982). *Father and child: Developmental and clinical perspectives.* Boston: Little, Brown.

Davie, R., Butler, N., & Goldstein, H. (1972). *From birth to seven. A report of the National Child Development Study.* London: Longman Group.

Dohrenwend, B.A., & Dohrenwend, B.P. (1974). *Stressful life events: Their nature and effects.* New York: Wiley.

Dunham, H.W. (1977). *Schizophrenia: The impact of sociocultural factors.* New York: Hospital Practice.

Erickson, E.H. (1950). *Childhood and society.* New York: W.W. Norton.

Fraiberg, S. (1977). *Every child's birthright.* New York: Basic Books.

Glick, I., & Kersler, D. (1974). *Marital and family therapy.* New York: Grune & Stratton.

Golding, W. (1959). *Lord of the flies.* New York: Putnam.

Greenspan, S.I. (1981). *Psychopathology and adaptation in infancy and early childhood: Principles of clinical diagnosis and preventive intervention.* New York: International Universities Press.

Grunebaum, H. (1977). Children at risk for psychosis and their families: Approaches to prevention. In M. McMillan & S. Henso (Eds.), *Child psychiatry: Treatment and research.* New York: Brunner/Mazel.

Hill, R. (1986). Life cycle stages for types of single parent families: Of family development theory. *Family Relations, 35,* 19–29.

Huygen, F.J.A. (1982). *Family medicine: The medical life histories of families.* New York: Brunner/Mazel.

Kaslow, F.W. (1981). Profile of the healthy family. *Interaction 4* (1, 2), 1–15.

Keniston, K., & Carnegie Council on Children. (1977). *All our children.* New York: Harcourt Brace Jovanovich.

Klaus, M.H., & Kennell, J.H. (1976). *Maternal-infant bonding.* St. Louis: C.V. Mosby.

Levy, D. (1958). *Behavioral analysis—Analysis of clinical observations of behavior, as applied to mother-newborn relationships.* Springfield, IL: CC Thomas.

Lidz, T. (1976). *The person* (rev. ed.). New York: Basic Books.

Lidz, T., & Fleck, S. (1985). *Schizophrenia and the Family* (rev. ed.). New York: International Universities Press.

Lindemann, E. (1979). *Beyond grief: Studies in crisis intervention.* New York: Aronson.

Lynn, D.B. (1979). *Daughters and parents: Past, present and future.* Monterey, CA: Brooks/Cole.

Miller, W.B., & Newman, L.F. (1978). *The first child and family formation.* Chapel Hill, NC: Carolina Population Center, University of North Carolina.

Nadelson, C., Notman, M., & Ellis, B.A. (1985). Psychosomatic aspects of obstetrics and gynecology. In W. Dorfman & L. Cristo (Eds.), *Psychosomatic illness review.* New York: Macmillan.

Offer, D., & Sabshin, M. (Eds.) (1984) *Normality and the life cycle.* New York: Basic Books.

Olson, L. (1983). *Costs of children.* Lexington, MA: Lexington Books.

Parsons, T., & Bales, R. (1955). *Family, socialization and interaction processes.* New York: Free Press.

Piaget, J. (1954). *The construction of reality in the child.* New York: Basic Books.

Provence, S., & Lipton, R.C. (1967). *Infants in institutions.* New York: International Universities Press.

Rainwater, L. (1965). *Family design.* Chicago: Aldine.

Reiss, D. (1981). *The family's construction of reality.* Cambridge, MA: Harvard University Press.

Saunders, C. (1959). *Care of the dying.* London: Macmillan.

Spitz, R. (1946). Anaclitic depression. *Psychoanalytic Studies of the Child, 2,* 313–342.

Spock, B. (1961). *Baby and child care.* New York: Pocket Books.

Stern, D. (1977). *The first relationship: Infant and mother.* Cambridge, MA: Harvard University Press.

Straus, M.A., Gelles, R.J., & Steinmetz, S.K. (1980). *Behind closed doors.* New York: Anchor Books.

Sze, W.C. (Ed.) (1975). *Human life cycle.* New York: Jason Aronson.

Vaillant, G.E. (1977). *Adaptation to life.* Boston: Little, Brown.

Wallerstein, J.S., & Kelly, J.B. (1980). *Surviving the breakup: How children and parents cope with divorce.* New York: Basic Books.

Werner, E.E., & Smith, R.S. (1982). *Vulnerable but invincible: A study of resilient children.* New York: McGraw-Hill.

Winnicott, D.W. (1965). *The family and individual development.* New York: Basic Books.

Zigler, E., & Gordon, E. (Eds.) (1982). *Day care: Scientific and social policy issues.* Boston: Auburn House.

INDEX

GAP COMMITTEES AND MEMBERSHIP

COMMITTEE ON ADOLESCENCE
Clarice J. Kestenbaum, New York, NY,
  Chairperson
Hector R. Bird, New York, NY
Ian A. Canino, New York, NY
Warren J. Gadpaille, Denver, CO
Michael G. Kalogerakis, New York, NY
Paulina F. Kernberg, New York, NY
Richard C. Marohn, Chicago, IL
Silvio J. Onesti, Jr., Belmont, MA

COMMITTEE ON AGING
Gene D. Cohen, Washington, DC
  Chairperson
Eric D. Caine, Rochester, NY
Charles M. Gaitz, Houston, TX
Ira R. Katz, Philadelphia, PA
Gabe J. Maletta, Minneapolis, MN
Robert J. Nathan, Philadelphia, PA
George H. Pollock, Chicago, IL
Kenneth M. Sakauye, New Orleans, LA
Charles A. Shamoian, Larchmont, NY
F. Conyers Thompson, Jr., Atlanta, GA

COMMITTEE ON ALCOHOLISM AND THE
  ADDICTIONS
Edward J. Khantzian, Haverhill, MA,
  Chairperson
Margaret H. Bean-Bayog, Lexington,
  MA
Richard J. Frances, Newark, NJ
Marc Galanter, New York, NY
Sheldon I. Miller, Newark, NJ
Robert B. Millman, New York, NY
Steven M. Mirin, Westwood, MA

Edgar P. Nace, Dallas, TX
Norman L. Paul, Lexington, MA
Peter Steinglass, Washington, DC
John S. Tamerin, Greenwich, CT

COMMITTEE ON CHILD PSYCHIATRY
Theodore Shapiro, New York, NY,
  Chairperson
James M. Bell, Canaan, NY
Harlow Donald Dunton, New York, NY
Joseph Fischhoff, Detroit, MI
Joseph M. Green, Madison, WI
John F. McDermott, Jr., Honolulu, HI
John Schowalter, New Haven, CT
Peter E. Tanguay, Los Angeles, CA
Leonore Terr, San Francisco, CA

COMMITTEE ON COLLEGE STUDENTS
Myron B. Liptzin, Chapel Hill, NC,
  Chairperson
Robert L. Arnstein, Hamden, CT
Varda Backus, La Jolla, CA
Harrison P. Eddy, New York, NY
Malkah Tolpin Notman, Brookline,
  MA
Gloria C. Onque, Pittsburgh, PA
Elizabeth Aub Reid, Cambridge, MA
Earle Silber, Chevy Chase, MD
Tom G. Stauffer, White Plains, NY

COMMITTEE ON CULTURAL PSYCHIATRY
Ezra E.H. Griffith, New Haven, CT,
  Chairperson
Edward F. Foulks, New Orleans, LA

Pedro Ruiz, Houston, TX
Ronald M. Wintrob, Providence, RI
Joe Yamamoto, Los Angeles, CA

COMMITTEE ON THE FAMILY
Herta A. Guttman, Toronto, Ont.,
  Chairperson
W. Robert Beavers, Dallas, TX
Ellen M. Berman, Merrion, PA
Lee Combrinck-Graham, Evanston,
  IL
Ira D. Glick, New York, NY
Frederick Gottlieb, Los Angeles, CA
Henry U. Grunebaum, Cambridge,
  MA
Ann L. Price, Hartford, CT
Lyman C. Wynne, Rochester, NY

COMMITTEE ON GOVERNMENTAL
  AGENCIES
Roger Peele, Washington, DC,
  Chairperson
Mark Blotcky, Dallas, TX
James P. Cattell, San Diego, CA
Thomas L. Clannon, San Francisco,
  CA
Sidney S. Goldensohn, New York, NY
Naomi Heller, Washington, DC
John P. D. Shemo, Charlottesville, VA
William W. Van Stone, Palo
  Alto, CA

COMMITTEE ON HANDICAPS
William H. Sack, Portland, OR,
  Chairperson
Norman R. Bernstein, Cambridge,
  MA
Meyer S. Gunther, Wilmette, IL
Betty J. Pfefferbaum, Houston, TX
William A. Sonis, Philadelphia, PA
Margaret L. Stuber, Los Angeles, CA
George Tarjan, Los Angeles, CA
Thomas G. Webster, Washington, DC
Henry H. Work, Bethesda, MD

COMMITTEE ON HUMAN SEXUALITY
Bertram H. Schaffner, New York, NY,
  Chairperson
Paul L. Adams, Galveston, TX
Johanna A. Hoffman, Scottsdale, AZ
Joan A. Lang, Galveston, TX
Stuart E. Nichols, New York, NY
Harris B. Peck, New Rochelle, NY
John P. Spiegel, Waltham, MA
Terry S. Stein, East Lansing, MI

COMMITTEE ON INTERNATIONAL
  RELATIONS
Vamik D. Volkan, Charlottesville, VA,
  Chairperson
Francis F. Barnes, Washington, DC
Robert M. Dorn, El Macero, CA
John S. Kafka, Washington, DC
Otto F. Kernberg, White Plains, NY
John E. Mack, Chestnut Hill, MA
Rita R. Rogers, Palos Verdes Estates, CA
Stephen B. Shanfield, San Antonio, TX

COMMITTEE ON MEDICAL EDUCATION
Stephen C. Scheiber, Deerfield, IL,
  Chairperson
Charles M. Culver, Hanover, NH
Steven L. Dubovsky, Denver, CO
Saul I. Harrison, Torrance, CA
David R. Hawkins, Chicago, IL
Harold I. Lief, Philadelphia, PA
Carol Nadelson, Boston, MA
Carolyn B. Robinowitz, Washington,
  DC
Sidney L. Werkman, Washington, DC
Veva H. Zimmerman, New York, NY

COMMITTEE ON MENTAL HEALTH
  SERVICES
Jose Maria Santiago, Tucson, AZ,
  Chairperson
Robert O. Friedel, Richmond, VA
John M. Hamilton, Columbia, MD
W. Walter Menninger, Topeka, KS

COMMITTEE ON RESEARCH
Robert Cancro, New York, NY,
  Chairperson
Kenneth Z. Altshuler, Dallas, TX
Jack A. Grebb, New York, NY
John H. Greist, Madison, WI
Jerry M. Lewis, Dallas, TX
Morris A. Lipton, Chapel Hill, NC
John G. Looney, Durham, NC
Sidney Malitz, New York, NY
Zebulon Taintor, New York, NY

COMMITTEE ON SOCIAL ISSUES
Ian E. Alger, New York, NY,
  Chairperson
William R. Beardslee, Waban, MA
Judith H. Gold, Halifax, N. S.
Roderic Gorney, Los Angeles, CA
Martha J. Kirkpatrick, Los Angeles,
  CA
Perry Ottenberg, Philadelphia, PA
Kendon W. Smith, Pearl River, NY

COMMITTEE ON THERAPEUTIC CARE
Donald W. Hammersley, Washington,
  DC, Chairperson
Bernard Bandler, Cambridge, MA
Thomas E. Curtis, Chapel Hill, NC
William B. Hunter, III, Albuquerque,
  NM
Roberto L. Jimenez, San Antonio, TX
Milton Kramer, Cincinnati, OH
Theodore Nadelson, Jamaica Plain,
  MA
William W. Richards, Anchorage, AK

COMMITTEE ON THERAPY
Allen D. Rosenblatt, La Jolla, CA,
  Chairperson
Jules R. Bemporad, Boston, MA
Henry W. Brosin, Tucson, AZ
Eugene B. Feigelson, Brooklyn, NY
Robert Michels, New York, NY
Andrew P. Morrison, Cambridge, MA
William C. Offenkrantz, Carefree, AZ

CONTRIBUTING MEMBERS
Gene Abroms, Ardmore, PA
John E. Adams, Gainesville, FL
Carlos C. Alden, Jr., Buffalo, NY
Spencer Bayles, Houston, TX
C. Christian Beels, New York, NY
Elissa P. Benedek, Ann Arbor, MI
Sidney Berman, Washington, DC
H. Keith H. Brodie, Durham, NC
Charles M. Bryant, San Francisco, CA
Ewald W. Busse, Durham, NC
Robert N. Butler, New York, NY
Eugene M. Caffey, Jr., Bowie, MD
Ian L.W. Clancey, Maitland, Ont.
Sanford I. Cohen, Coral Gables, FL
Paul E. Dietz, Newport Beach, CA
James S. Eaton, Jr., Washington, DC
Lloyd C. Elam, Nashville, TN
Stanley H. Eldred, Belmont, MA
Joseph T. English, New York, NY
Louis C. English, Pomona, NY
Sherman C. Feinstein, Highland Park,
  IL
Archie R. Foley, New York, NY
Sidney Furst, Bronx, NY
Henry J. Gault, Highland Park, IL
Alexander Gralnick, Port Chester, NY
Milton Greenblatt, Sylmar, CA
Lawrence F. Greenleigh, Los Angeles,
  CA
Stanley I. Greenspan, Bethesda, MD
Jon E. Gudeman, Milwaukee, WI
Stanley Hammons, Lexington, KY
William Hetznecker, Merion Station, PA
J. Cotter Hirschberg, Topeka, KS
Jay Katz, New Haven, CT
James A. Knight, New Orleans, LA
Othilda M. Krug, Cincinnati, OH
Judith Landau-Stanton, Rochester, NY
Alan I. Levenson, Tucson, AZ
Ruth W. Lidz, Woodbridge, CT
Orlando B. Lightfoot, Boston, MA
Norman L. Loux, Sellersville, PA
Albert J. Lubin, Woodside, CA
John A. MacLeod, Cincinnati, OH
Leo Madow, Philadelphia, PA
Charles A. Malone, Barrington, RI

GAP Reports Published by Brunner/Mazel, Inc.

Crisis of Adolescence—Teenage Pregnancy: Impact on Adolescent Development, Report #118

A Family Affair: Helping Families Cope with Mental Illness: A Guide for the Professions, Report #119

The Family, the Patient, and the Psychiatric Hospital: Toward a New Model, Report #117

How Old Is Old Enough? The Ages of Rights and Responsibilities, Report #126

Interactive Fit: A Guide to Nonpsychotic Chronic Patients, Report #121

The Psychiatric Treatment of Alzheimer's Disease, Report #125

Psychiatry and the Mental Health Professionals: New Roles for Changing Times, Report #122

Research and the Complex Causality of the Schizophrenias, Report #116

Speaking Out for Psychiatry: A Handbook for Involvement with the Mass Media, Report #124

Teaching Psychotherapy in Contemporary Psychiatric Residency Training, Report #120

Us and Them: The Psychology of Ethnonationalism, Report #123

*For ordering information
and a complete listing of available reports*

Brunner/Mazel, Inc.
19 Union Square West, New York, NY 10003
212-924-3344

DATE DUE

DEMCO 38-297